D1488176

Que® Quick Reference Series

WordPerfect® 5.1
Quick Reference

Developed by
Que Corporation

Que® Corporation
Carmel, Indiana

WordPerfect 5.1 Quick Reference.

Library of Congress Catalog Number: 90-60372

ISBN 0-88022-576-9

93   92   15 14 13 12

Interpretation of the printing code: the rightmost double-digit number is the year of the book's printing; the rightmost single-digit number is the number of the book's printing. For example, a printing code of 90-4 shows that the fourth printing of the book occurred in 1990.

This book is based on WordPerfect 5.1 and the earlier Version 5.0.

Que Quick Reference Series

The *Que Quick Reference Series* is a portable resource of essential microcomputer knowledge. Whether you are a new or experienced user, you can rely on the high-quality information contained in these convenient guides.

Drawing on the experience of many of Que's best-selling authors, the *Que Quick Reference Series* helps you easily access important program information.

Now it's easy to look up often-used commands and functions for 1-2-3, dBASE IV, WordPerfect 5, Microsoft Word 5, and MS-DOS, as well as programming information for C, Turbo Pascal, and QuickBASIC 4.

Use the *Que Quick Reference Series* as a compact alternative to confusing and complicated traditional documentation.

The *Que Quick Reference Series* includes these titles:

1-2-3 Quick Reference
1-2-3 Release 2.2 Quick Reference
1-2-3 Release 3 Quick Reference
Assembly Language Quick Reference
AutoCAD Quick Reference
C Quick Reference
dBASE IV Quick Reference
DOS and BIOS Functions Quick Reference
Excel Quick Reference
Hard Disk Quick Reference
Harvard Graphics Quick Reference
MS-DOS Quick Reference
Microsoft Word 5 Quick Reference
Norton Utilities Quick Reference
PC Tools Quick Reference
QuickBASIC Quick Reference
Turbo Pascal Quick Reference
WordPerfect Quick Reference
WordPerfect 5.1 Quick Reference

Publishing Director
Lloyd J. Short

Product Director
Karen A. Bluestein

Production Editor
Cheryl Robinson

Editor
Sandra Blackthorn

Technical Editor
Ron Holmes

Indexer
Hilary Adams

Production
Corinne Harmon
Jennifer Matthews
Bruce D. Steed
Nora Westlake

Table of Contents

Introduction

WordPerfect 5.1 Quick Reference is not a rehash of traditional documentation. Instead, this quick reference is a compilation of the most frequently used information from Que's best-selling WordPerfect books.

WordPerfect 5.1 Quick Reference presents essential information on WordPerfect commands, functions, and macros. You will learn the proper use of primary WordPerfect functions, as well as how to avoid serious errors. This book contains fundamental information in a compact, easy-to-use format, but is not intended as a replacement for the comprehensive information presented in a full-size guide. You should supplement this quick reference with one of Que's complete WordPerfect texts, such as *WordPerfect Quickstart, Using WordPerfect 5.1,* or *WordPerfect Tips, Tricks and Traps.*

WordPerfect 5.1 Quick Reference is divided into sections. The Command Reference is an alphabetical listing of all WordPerfect commands. Each command is presented in the same format. A brief introductory paragraph provides an explanation of each command. The Procedures sections provide step-by-step instructions. Periodically throughout the book, you will find Reminders. These reminders serve to advise you of other tips that will help you use WordPerfect 5.1's features successfully.

Now you can put essential information at your fingertips with *WordPerfect 5.1 Quick Reference*—and the entire Que Quick Reference Series!

HINTS FOR USING THIS BOOK

WordPerfect 5.1 Quick Reference is task-oriented—which means that it is oriented to your needs, not the structure of the program. Because topics are arranged alphabetically, begin with what you want to accomplish. For example, if you want information on how to set up newspaper-style columns, look under Columns.

Within each section, subheadings help you find the information you need. For instance, within the Columns section you will find information on newspaper-style columns, parallel columns, and editing columns. Some sections contain reminders to help you perform the tasks.

The type conventions used in this book have been established to help you execute WordPerfect commands. Commands or words you type appear in boldfaced type. On-screen messages appear in a special digital typeface. For function-key commands, the keystrokes are presented first, followed by the name of the command.

FEATURES NEW TO WORDPERFECT 5.1

Version 5.1 offers nearly a dozen new features, which are summarized in the following chart:

New Feature	Summary
Dormant hard returns	The first hard return code after a soft-page code is made dormant; the blank line that normally results is suppressed.

Equations	Complex equations can be entered using common terms and symbols.
Labels	Can be defined as a paper type and easily enter information for continuous-feed or sheet labels.
Long document names	Can be up to 68 characters or spaces.
Printing	Can print document summaries or selected pages of on-screen document. Added support for double-sided printing.
Pull-down menus and mouse support	Pull-down menus available and supports use of mouse.
Keyboard layouts	Comes with several key boards that use macros for quick cursor movement, code editing, and equation entry.
Special characters	Supports more than 1,500 characters.
Spreadsheet Import and Linking	Brings spreadsheets directly to 5.1. Changes in spreadsheets also update documents.
Tables	Simple definition and formatting of tables, including use of simple math calculations.
Text Drivers	Support added for monitors that support extended text modes.

COMMAND REFERENCE

Following is an alphabetical listing of command tasks. Instructions for specific procedures appear under the appropriate task headings.

Adding Text

WordPerfect normally operates in *Insert mode*. In Insert mode, new characters are inserted, and existing text moves forward and is automatically formatted. As you type, sentences may push beyond the right margin and may not immediately wrap to the next line. Don't worry. The lines adjust as you continue to type.

Typeover mode generally is used if you type text incorrectly. For example, you probably would select Typeover mode if you mistakenly typed the name *Jane* rather than *Dane*.

Remember that Typeover mode *replaces* original text; Insert mode *adds* new text to existing text.

To add text by using Insert mode

1. Place the cursor where you want to insert new text.

2. Type the new text

To add text by typing over existing text

1. Place the cursor where you want the new text to begin.

2. Press Ins to turn off Insert mode.

3. Type the new text.

4. Press Ins again to return to Insert mode.

Block Command

One of the most powerful and flexible commands in WordPerfect is the Block command (Alt-F4 or F12 on the Enhanced Keyboard). Use this command with other features to block (isolate) specific segments of text so that only the blocked text is affected by those features.

Blocks can be a single character, a single word, a phrase, a sentence, a paragraph, a page, a column, a rectangle of text of any size, or a document.

On-screen, blocked text appears highlighted. After the text is highlighted, it is ready for the second step in a variety of operations.

Some WordPerfect features cannot be used with the Block command. For example, to change margin settings in a portion of your document, you use the Format Line command, not the Block command.

Defining a Block

Before you do anything to a block of text, you must use the Block command to define the block of text by highlighting it on-screen.

To define a block of text

1. Move the cursor to the character that begins the block of text you want to define.

2. Press Alt-F4 or F12 to begin the Block command.

3. Move the cursor to the right until the last character in the block of text is highlighted.

   Use the cursor-movement keys, PgDn, PgUp, and GoTo (Ctrl-Home) keys to move the cursor. You can move the cursor either forward or backward to define text. The highlight moves with the cursor.

Type any character to advance the block to the next occurrence of that character.

4. Press the key that invokes the feature you plan to use on the highlighted block of text.

   To back out of the feature while the block is highlighted, press F1 (Cancel), or Alt-F4 or F12 (Block), to turn off the Block command. The Block on message disappears, and the text no longer appears highlighted. The cursor remains at the end of the block.

   Some commands, such as Block Print or Block Delete, require confirmation. If a Yes (No) prompt appears at the lower left of the screen, complete the next step.

5. Press Y to select Yes or press N for No.

   The feature you selected in Step 4 executes only on the highlighted block of text.

   To rehighlight the block for use with another feature or to restore highlighting if you accidentally turn off the Block feature, complete the next steps. (Note that this procedure works as long as you have not moved the cursor in the interim.)

6. Press Alt-F4 or F12 (Block).

7. Press Ctrl-Home (GoTo) to activate the GoTo command.

8. Press Ctrl-Home (GoTo) again to return to the beginning of the block.

Block highlighting disappears as soon as the task (such as move, copy, or bold) is completed.

Moving a Block

Moving a block of text is a "cut and paste" operation. You simply define the block, cut it from its current location, and move it to a new location. The block disappears from its previous location and reappears in the new location. The new location can be in another document.

To move a block of text

1. With **Alt-F4** or **F12**, define the block of text you want to move.

2. Press **Ctrl-F4** (**Move**) to display the Move menu

   ```
   Move: 1 Block; 2 Tabular Column;
   3 Rectangle: 0
   ```

   Note that if the block is a sentence, paragraph, or page, Step 1 can be omitted, and the preceding menu is replaced by the following menu:

   ```
   Move: 1 Sentence; 2 Paragraph; 3
   Page; 4 Retrieve: 0.
   ```

3. Press **1** or **B** to select Block.

4. Press **1** or **M** to select Move. WordPerfect cuts the defined block, and it disappears from the screen.

5. Move the cursor to where you want the block to appear.

6. Press **Enter** to insert the block at the new location.

Copying a Block

When you copy a block of text, WordPerfect places into memory a duplicate of the block you defined. You then can retrieve this block from memory and insert it at another location. To copy a block of text, use the Block command (**Alt-F4** or **F12**) with the Move command (**Ctrl-F4**).

To copy a block of text

1. With Alt-F4 or F12, define the block to be copied.

2. Press Ctrl-F4 (Move).

   Note: If the block is a sentence, paragraph, or page, Step 1 can be omitted, and a different menu appears.)

3. Press 1 or B to select Block.

4. Press 2 or C to select Copy. The highlighting disappears.

5. Move the cursor to where you want the duplicate text to appear.

6. Press Enter.

Deleting a Block

Block Delete is the most efficient way to delete more than one or two characters.

To delete a block of text

1. With Alt-F4 or F12, define the block you want deleted.

2. Press the Del key or the Backspace key.

3. Press Y. (If you press N, you return to the highlighted text.) The block is deleted from your document.

You can delete as many as three blocks and restore them all using the Undelete (F1) feature.

Restoring a Block

To restore deleted text

1. Press F1 (Cancel/Undelete) to display the most recently deleted text.

2. Press 1 or R to restore the text to your document or press 2 , P, ↑, or ↓ to display the previous deletion.

If the previous deletion is the text you want restored, press 1; if not, press 2 again to view the third, and last, deletion.

Saving a Block

WordPerfect's Block Save function helps reduce the amount of work when you must type the same block of text in one document several times.

To save a block of text

1. With Alt-F4 or F12, define the block you want to save.

2. Press F10 (Save).

   Note: If you use Ctrl-F4 to highlight a sentence, paragraph, or page, you then choose 4 (Append). The prompt append to: appears.

3. Type the name of the file in which you want to save the block.

   Select a file name that clearly identifies the block. Be sure to include a drive letter and path name before the file name if you want to save the block to a directory other than the current directory.

4. Press Enter.

Printing a Block

Sometimes you will want to print only a single block of text from a document.

To print a block of text

1. With Alt-F4 or F12, define the block you plan to print.

2. Press Shift-F7 (Print).

3. In response to the prompt, press Y.

Appending a Block

WordPerfect provides a way for you to add text to one document as you work on another—using the Block Append command. With Append, the text is attached to the end of the document.

To append a block of text

1. With Alt-F4 or F12, define the text you plan to append.

2. Press Ctrl-F4 (Move).

3. Press 1 or B for Block.

4. Press 4 or A for Append.

5. Type the file name of the document to which you want to append the block. The block remains in your current document and is added to the end of your other document.

Changing Block Case

To change upper- or lowercase

1. With Alt-F4 or F12, define the block you plan to change to upper- or lowercase letters.

2. Press Shift-F3 (Switch).

3. Press 1 or U to change the block to uppercase letters or press 2 or L to change the block to lowercase letters.

Centering a Block of Text

To center a block of text

1. With Alt-F4 or F12, define the block of text you want to center.

2. Press Shift-F6 (Center).

3. Press Y to center the block. The block is centered between the left and right margins.

Enhancing a Block of Text

To boldface or underline a block of text

1. With Alt-F4 or F12 (Block), define the block of text you want to boldface or underline.

2. Press F6 to turn on Bold or F8 to turn on Underline.

If you want the block to be both boldfaced and underlined, highlight the block again by pressing Alt-F4 or F12 (Block) and then press Ctrl-Home (GoTo) twice. Press F6 (Bold) or F8 (Underline), depending on which you used the first time.

Cancel/Undelete

The Cancel/Undelete key (the F1 "oops" key) enables you to back out of a menu without making a selection or restore text you mistakenly deleted.

When used as a cancel key, F1 cancels the most recent command and returns you to the preceding menu or to your document. When used as an undelete key, F1 displays one of the last three items you deleted. An *item* in this case means the characters (numbers, letters, codes, or punctuation) deleted before the cursor was moved. F1 always acts as an undelete key when a menu is not active.

To back out of a menu

Press F1 (Cancel) to return to a preceding menu without making a choice from the current menu. When there is no preceding menu to which to return, you return to the current document.

Some menus disregard your selections if you leave the menu by pressing the Cancel key (F1). These menus display a message that instructs you to leave the menu by pressing the Exit key (F7) if you want to save your selections in memory.

Restoring Deleted Text

Press F1 (Cancel) to display deleted text either in its original location or to another location. You then can restore the text, if you want.

Remember that WordPerfect stores only the last three deletions. When you make a fourth deletion, the oldest of the three preceding deletions is erased from memory.

Deleted text is not saved when you exit WordPerfect. To save text, you must paste it into a document and save the document.

To restore deleted text or codes

1. Move the cursor to the location where the deleted item should reappear. If you just deleted the text and want it returned to its original location, do not move the cursor.

2. Press F1 (Cancel) to display the Undelete menu and the text you last deleted. The last deletion shows as highlighted text at the cursor's location. At this point, you have three options: (a) press F1 (Cancel) or Enter if you want to return to typing without restoring the text; (b) press 1 or R for Restore if you want to restore the deleted text to your document; or (c) press 2 , P, ↑, or ↓ for Previous Deletion until the text you want to restore is displayed and then press 1 or R for Restore.

Clearing a Document

You must clear the current document from the screen before you start work on a new document—unless you want to combine them.

Reminders

If you do not clear the current document before starting a new document or before retrieving a document from memory, the old and the new documents merge to form a continuous (and perhaps confusing) document.

Caution: *Never* turn off your computer (or remove your working copy of the 5 1/4-inch WordPerfect 2 disk or the 3 1/2-inch WordPerfect 1/WordPerfect 2 [sys] disk from the disk drive) before you clear the current document from the screen and exit to DOS. You will know that you have returned to DOS when you see the DOS prompt (A>, B>, or C>) on-screen (unless you are using a menu shell).

To clear the current document

1. Press F7 (Exit).

2. Press Y to begin the save process.

3. Type the file name and press Enter. If the document already exists, WordPerfect prompts

   ```
   Replace (file name)? No (Yes)
   ```

4. Press Y to save the document with the old name, or press N and repeat Step 3. Your document is stored under the name you select. For easy retrieval, use descriptive file names.

If you don't want to save the document you created, or if you saved the document previously but you want to clear your screen, follow these steps:

1. Press F7 (Exit).

2. Press N.

In response to the prompt, either press Y (to exit WordPerfect and return to DOS) or press N or Enter to clear the screen. If you press F1 (Cancel), you are returned to the document displayed on-screen.

Columns

Newspaper-Style Columns

Newspaper-style columns are read from top to bottom. The text flows from the bottom of one column to the top of the next. Newspaper-style columns are used for magazine articles, newsletters, lists, and indexes.

To define newspaper-style columns

1. Move the cursor to the position where you want columns to begin.

2. Press Alt-F7 (Columns/Table).

3. Press 1 or C to select Columns; then press 3 or D to choose Define and display the Text Column Definition menu. The default is Newspaper with

two columns of equal width and a half-inch gutter between the columns. Press Enter to accept the setting.

If you want more than two columns, press 2 or N to choose Number of Columns. You do not need   to press 1 for Type because Newspaper is WordPerfect's default setting.

4. Enter the number of columns you want on your page (up to 24) and then press Enter.

5. Press 3 or D for Distance Between Columns. WordPerfect automatically calculates the margin settings, with one-half inch between columns, but you can space your columns as you want.

   In most cases, you will accept the default margin settings. If you plan to use columns of different widths, however, you must type the margin specifications.

6. To accept the default margin settings, press Enter To enter new settings manually, press 4 or M to choose Margins and then enter the new settings for Left and Right column margins. Be sure to press Enter after each number.

7. Press F7 (Exit) to accept the settings and press F7 again to exit the Text Column Definition menu.

8. Press 1 or O to turn on columns.

9. Begin typing. Your text wraps within the column until you reach the bottom of the page and then wraps to the top of the next column.

10. To turn off columns, press Alt-F7 (Columns/ Table), press 1 or C for Columns, and press 2 or F for Column On/Off and turn columns off.

After you turn off columns, any text you type is formatted as a normal document, and the column number disappears from the status line.

Parallel Columns

Parallel columns are read from left to right across the page. For example, parallel columns are used in a script in which names or brief instructions are typed in the first column and words to be spoken are typed in the second column. Inventory lists often are set up in parallel columns, as are personnel rosters and duty schedules.

You type text into parallel columns by moving from column to column across the page.

To define parallel columns

1. Press Alt-F7 (Columns/Table).

2. Press 3 or D to choose Define.

3. Press 1 or T to select Type.

4. Press 2 or P to select Parallel or press 3 or B to select Parallel with Block Protect.

   Parallel with Block Protect prevents a horizontal block of text from being split by a soft page break. When a column (other than the last column) reaches the bottom margin, the entire block of columns is moved to the next page.

   If a block of columns is longer than a page, Block Protect is turned off and text continues in the same column on the next page.

5. Press 2 or N to choose Number of Columns, if necessary.

6. Type the desired number of columns and press Enter.

7. Press 3 or D for Distance Between Columns and press Enter. If you want to specify a distance between columns that differs from WordPerfect's default (one-half inch), enter a new specification and press Enter.

8. Press 4 or M to choose Margins, enter margin specifications, and press Enter.

9. Press F7 (Exit) to return to the Math/Columns menu and then press 1 or O to turn columns On.

To enter column headings

1. Press Shift-F6 (Center) and type the column heading.

2. Press Ctrl-Enter (Hard Page) to move to the next column and press Shift-F6 (Center).

3. Type the heading.

4. Repeat Steps 1–3 until all the column headings have been entered.

5. Press Ctrl-Enter (Hard Page) after the last column heading is typed. The cursor rests at the first column location at the left of your page.

To enter text into parallel columns

1. With the cursor positioned at the left margin, type the text for the first column.

2. When you finish typing a column entry, press Ctrl-Enter (Hard Page) and move to the next column.

3. Repeat Steps 1 and 2 for the other columns.

4. When you finish typing text under the last column heading, press Ctrl-Enter (Hard Page) to return the cursor to the left margin. You can begin typing the next group of column entries. WordPerfect inserts one blank line to separate the groups of text.

To create an empty column, press Ctrl-Enter (Hard Page) twice.

Editing Columns

In Column mode, the editing keys work as explained in the following table.

The Editing Keys in Column Mode

Editing Key(s)	Function
Ctrl-End	Erases to the end of the line in the column being edited.
Ctrl-PgDn	Erases to the end of the column starting at the cursor position.
→	Moves the cursor to the right within the current column.
←	Moves the cursor to the left within the current column.
↑	Scrolls all columns.
↓	Scrolls all columns.
Ctrl-Home, →	Moves the cursor to the next column.
Ctrl-Home, ←	Moves the cursor to the previous column.
Home, ↑	Moves the cursor to the top of the column on the current screen.
Home, ↓	Moves the cursor to the bottom of the column on the current screen.
Ctrl-Home, ← or →	Moves the cursor to the first or last column.

Comparing Documents

WordPerfect can compare the new version of a document with an old version if you saved a copy to disk under another name. Sections of the on-screen document that don't exist in the disk file are redlined. Text that exists in the disk file, but not in the on-screen document, is copied to the on-screen document and marked with strikeout.

To compare documents

1. Press Alt-F5 (Mark Text). The following menu appears:

   ```
   1 Cross Ref; 2 Subdoc; 3 Index;
   4 ToA Short Form; 5 Define; 6
   Generate: 0
   ```

2. Press 6 or G to choose Generate.

3. Press 2 or C to choose Compare Screen and Disk Documents and Add Redline and Strikeout.

4. Type the name of the file you want to compare with the on-screen document.

WordPerfect compares the documents, inserting Redline and Strikeout codes. If a section of text has been moved, WordPerfect marks the affected text with Strikeout and inserts the highlighted message THE FOLLOWING TEXT WAS MOVED before the text and THE PRECEDING TEXT WAS MOVED after the text.

To remove redline and strikeout

1. Press Alt-F5 (Mark Text).

2. Press 6 or G to choose Generate.

3. Press 1 or R to choose Remove Redline Markings and Strikeout Text from Document.

4. Press **Y** to remove redline and strikeout, or press **N** to leave redline and strikeout and return to the document.

5. Save your document again.

After you press **Y**, all Redline codes are removed. Strikeout codes *and the text between them* are removed.

Cross-References

To guide your readers to related information in the document, you can use WordPerfect's Cross-Reference feature to reference page numbers, footnote numbers, section numbers, endnote numbers, and graphics box numbers. If you make changes, the references are renumbered automatically.

You create an automatic reference using two types of codes: a *reference code* marks the place you make the reference, and a *target code* marks the place to which you refer. For example, on page 10, if you refer to related information on page 20, place the reference code on page 10 and the target code on page 20.

To mark both the reference and the target

1. Move the cursor to the position where you want to create an automatic reference.

2. Type the introductory text, such as Refer to page #, and press the space bar.

3. Press Alt-F5 (Mark Text) .

4. Press 1 or R to choose Cross-Ref and display the Mark Text: Cross-Reference menu.

5. Press 3 or B to choose Mark Both Reference and Target. The Tie Reference To menu appears.

6. Type the number that represents the type of target for the reference you are creating. (If you select Graphics Box Number, select the type of box you are referencing from the menu.)

7. Move your cursor to the target and press Enter.

8. Type a name for the target and press Enter.

WordPerfect marks the reference, as well as the target, with the name you select for the target. When you press Enter, WordPerfect returns the cursor to the position of the Reference code and inserts the target page number.

Instead of marking the reference and the target at the same time, you can mark each separately.

To mark the reference only

1. Follow Steps 1–4 for marking both the reference and the target.

2. Press 1 or R to choose Mark Reference.

3. Type the number of the type of target.

4. Type a name for the target and press Enter.

In the reference code, WordPerfect enters a question mark. When you name a target with the same name you chose for this reference and generate the references, WordPerfect replaces the question mark with the number of the target.

To mark the target only

1. Follow Steps 1–4 for marking both the reference and the target.

2. Press 2 or T to choose Mark Target.

3. Type a name for the target and press Enter.

WordPerfect generates reference numbers when you enter a reference and target at the same time. But, if you mark targets and references separately, or if you make editing changes, you need to generate references to update the reference numbers.

To generate automatic references, press Alt-F5 (Mark Text) and press 6 or G to choose Generate.

Cursor Movement

The *cursor* is the blinking underline character that marks the location on the screen where the next character you type will appear. The cursor also marks the location in your text where codes (such as those used for creating new margin settings) will be entered.

As the cursor reaches the right margin at the end of the line, WordPerfect's automatic return feature (called *word wrap*) returns the cursor to the beginning of the next line so that you can continue without interruption.

You use the keys marked with arrows at the far right of the keyboard to control cursor movement. When you press an arrow key, the cursor moves in the direction indicated by the arrow on that key.

If you try to move the cursor with a cursor-arrow key on a blank screen, nothing happens. WordPerfect doesn't permit the cursor to move where nothing exists.

You move the cursor by pressing the arrow keys, PgUp, PgDn, +, −, or GoTo (Ctrl-Home); typing text; pressing the space bar; or pressing the Tab key.

All keys except the function keys and the cursor-arrow keys respond much like the keys on an electric typewriter—with a few special exceptions. The Alt and Ctrl keys are used in combination with other keys to provide WordPerfect capabilities that a single key cannot provide.

The Enter, or Return, key can be used as a carriage
return. You also press Enter to insert blank lines in your
text, such as the lines that separate paragraphs.

When the Num Lock key is activated, the cursor-
movement keys become the numeric keys used for
performing math functions.

Using PgUp and PgDn

Use the PgUp or PgDn keys to move the cursor a page at
a time. When you press one of these keys, the prompt
Repositioning flashes momentarily on the status line.

Using GoTo

Use GoTo (Ctrl-Home) to move to a specific page or
character in your document. Also use this command to
move between columns, to move to the top or bottom of
the page, and to move to the cursor's original position.

To move to a specific page or character

1. Check the page number on the status line.

2. Press Ctrl-Home (GoTo).

3. Type the number of the page or the character to
   which you want to move.

4. Press Enter. The cursor moves to the top of that
   page or to the immediate right of the first
   occurrence of that character.

To move between columns

1. Press Ctrl-Home (GoTo).

2. Press the left arrow to move the cursor to the
   previous column or press the right arrow to move
   the cursor to the next column.

To move to the top or bottom of the page

1. Press Ctrl-Home (GoTo).

2. Press the up arrow to move to the top of the page or press the down arrow to move to the bottom of the page.

To move to the cursor's original position

1. Press Ctrl-Home (GoTo).

2. Press Ctrl-Home (GoTo) again. The cursor returns to its original position within the document.

The cursor returns to its original position only after you use one of these features: Esc, GoTo, Home and arrow keys, PgUp and PgDn, Replace, Screen Up and Screen Down, and Search.

To move the cursor a specific number of lines or character spaces

1. Press Esc. The Repeat Value = 8 on your screen is WordPerfect's system default number, but you can move the cursor any number of lines.

2. Enter the number of lines you want to move.

3. Press the appropriate arrow key (up or down). The cursor moves in the direction indicated by the arrow key for exactly the number of lines you specify.

Cursor-Movement Keys

The following tables summarize the cursor-movement keys.

Horizontal Cursor-Movement Keys

Key(s)	Function
← or →	Character left or right codes.
Ctrl- →	Moves word right.

Ctrl- ←	Moves word left.
Home- ←	Moves to left edge of screen.
Home-→ or End	Moves to right end of line.
Home-Home- ←	Moves to far left of line.
Home-Home-Home- ←	Moves to far left of line (preceding all hidden command codes)
Ctrl-Home-*n*	Positions cursor after a specific character, *n*.
Tab	In insert mode, moves text right to next tab. In typeover mode, moves cursor to next tab.
Shift-Tab	Moves cursor to previous tab.
Backspace	In typeover mode, moves text left and enters a blank.

Vertical Cursor-Movement Keys

Key(s)	*Function*
↑ and ↓	Moves cursor up and down one line at a time.
Home- ↑ or minus (–) on numeric keypad	Moves cursor to top of screen.
Home- ↓ or plus (+) on numeric keypad	Moves cursor to bottom of screen.
Ctrl-Home- ↑	Moves cursor to top of current page.

Ctrl-Home- ↓	Moves cursor to end of current page.
PgUp	Moves cursor to top of preceding page.
PgDn	Moves cursor to top of next page.
Home-Home- ↑	Moves cursor to beginning of document.
Home-Home-Home- ↑	Moves cursor to beginning of document (preceding all hidden command codes).
Home-Home- ↓	Moves cursor to end of document.
Ctrl-Home-#-Enter	Moves to page #.
Esc-#- ↑	Moves # lines up.
Esc-#- ↓	Moves # lines down.

Customizing WordPerfect

When you install WordPerfect, you accept the default settings for features such as margin settings, keyboard layout, cursor speed, and so on. You can use the Setup menu (Shift-F1) to customize the system to fit your work environment. When you make a change, the new setting is permanent and affects every document you create until you use the Setup menu to change the defaults again. Existing documents are not affected. To change the defaults of an existing document, press Shift-F8, D, and C.

Using a Mouse

WordPerfect supports the use of a mouse. You can use the mouse to choose menu items, files from a list, and block text. The Setup menu's Mouse options enable you to select and fine-tune a mouse.

Mouse Type lets you tell WordPerfect the brand and model of mouse you are using. If your mouse is not listed, select Mouse Driver; then, *before* starting WordPerfect, run the MOUSE.COM program that came with your mouse.

Mouse Port lets you indicate which serial port your mouse is connected to. This option is ignored if you have a bus or PS/2 mouse.

Double Click Interval indicates the amount of time you have to select a menu choice by double-clicking. If you exceed the time interval, WordPerfect interprets your actions as two separate clicks.

Submenu Delay Time is how long the mouse must remain on a menu choice before any submenu appears.

Acceleration Factor lets you adjust the sensitivity of the mouse.

Left-Handed Mouse swaps the actions of the left and right mouse buttons for left-handed users.

Assisted Mouse Movement positions the mouse pointer to the first selectable item.

Adjusting the Display

The Display option on the Setup menu controls many aspects of WordPerfect's screen display. For example, you can change the color of normal text and various text attributes (if you have a color monitor), determine whether the current file name is displayed on the status line, select how menus and columns are shown on-screen, and so on.

You can change the following options on the Display menu:

Colors/Fonts/Attributes
Graphics Screen Type
Menu Options
Edit Screen Options

Each of these options brings up a menu with additional configuration choices. For example, when you select Edit Screen Options, you can set the following selections:

Automatically Format and Rewrite
Comments Display
Filename on the Status Line
Hard Return Display Character
Merge Codes Display
Reveal Codes Window Size
Side-by-Side Columns Display

Setting the Environment

With WordPerfect, you can select an operating environment that suits your work habits. You can set the following options to your liking.

WordPerfect's Setup menu offers two automatic backup options: Timed Backup and Original Backup. If you select the Timed Backup option, at specified intervals WordPerfect saves the document displayed on-screen. If you have documents in both windows (Doc 1 and Doc 2), only the active document is backed up. You must press F7 to save your work permanently. Setting the Original Backup option causes WordPerfect to save the original file each time you replace it with an edited version. The original document is renamed with the extension .BK!. Each time you replace the document with a new version, the .BK! file is replaced with the most recently edited version.

The Beep options enable you to tell WordPerfect whether it should beep when an error occurs, when manual hyphenation is required, or when a search operation does not find a match.

Choose the Cursor Speed option to make your cursor move faster or slower.

Use the Document Management/Summary option to control whether a document summary is created and whether WordPerfect uses its own long document naming scheme in addition to the DOS file name.

Files are saved more quickly with the Fast Save (unformatted) option, but you cannot print fast-saved files from the disk. Instead, you must retrieve the document to the screen and then print.

Choose External Rules to use WordPerfect's hyphenation dictionary or choose Internal Rules to use a "best guess" method based on grammar algorithms.

WordPerfect never prompts you for hyphenation. Always use the Prompt for Hyphenation option when you want to hyphenate words.

With the units of measure options, you can set WordPerfect to use inches, centimeters, points, WordPerfect 4.2 units, or its internal system of measurements.

Choosing Initial Settings

With Merge, you can tell WordPerfect how fields and records are separated in DOS text files. This option is especially useful for direct importation of dBASE or BASIC files.

Date Format determines the default appearance when you insert a date code into a document. An example of the default format fully spelled out is March 19, 1991.

With Equations, you can tell WordPerfect to print equations as graphics (to print math symbols your printer does not normally support), and you can determine whether equations should appear larger than surrounding text, how equations should be positioned vertically and horizontally within a graphics box, and whether you want to automatically redefine your keyboard when editing equations (WordPerfect supplies a predefined EQUATION.WPK keyboard layout).

Because WordPerfect saves the current printer information within the document file, the program must know how to handle a document that was saved while one printer was selected and then retrieved while another printer was selected. (This occurrence is common when several WordPerfect users who own different printers exchange files.) Use the Format Retrieved Documents for Default Printer option in this situation.

With the Initial Codes option, you can determine which codes always are inserted into a new document. If, for example, you want 1 1/2-inch left and right margins rather than WordPerfect's 1-inch default margins, enter the margin change here; then 1 1/2-inch margins are inserted into every document you create.

Repeat Value, which repeats certain actions such as cursor movement, is set to 8 at the factory.

You can enter several Table of Authorities options regarding the use of dot leaders, underlining, and blank lines between individual citations.

Print Options allows you to enter default values for Binding Offset, Number of Copies (and whether they are generated by WordPerfect or your printer), Graphics Quality, Text Quality, Redline Method, and Size Attribute Ratios for Fine, Small, Large, Very Large, Extra Large, and Super/Subscript fonts.

Determining File Location

Press **6** or **L** to tell WordPerfect where you intend to
store various types of files. You may, for example,
want to store your keyboard and macro files in
C:\WP51\MACROS, your printer files in
C:\WP51\PRINTER, and your documents in
C:\WP51\DOCS. These entries may contain information you entered during installation.

For a complete discussion of WordPerfect's customizing features, see Chapter 18 and Appendix A of
Que's *Using WordPerfect 5.1*.

Date and Time Codes

WordPerfect can check your computer's clock and insert
the current date and time in a document. The program
also can insert function codes that update the date and
time automatically every time you retrieve or print the
document.

Reminders

WordPerfect cannot insert the correct date and time
unless your computer's clock is set correctly. Check the
instruction manual for your computer to learn how to
reset the clock.

To insert date codes

1. Move the cursor to the position where you want to
   insert the date or time code.

2. Press **Shift-F5** (**Date/Outline**). WordPerfect
   displays the Date/Outline menu.

3. Press **1** or **T** to choose Date Text. WordPerfect
   immediately types the current date—July 19, 1990,
   for example. If you have set the Date/Time format

to include the time, the current time is also included—for example, July 19, 1990 — 10:32 am.

Or press 2 or C to choose Date Code. WordPerfect types the current date and inserts a code into your document—[Date:3 1, 4], for example. (The numbers in the code represent formatting parameters.)

Whenever you retrieve or print the document, Word-Perfect automatically updates the Date Code to the current date and time.

You can change the date/time format so that it enters text or codes for (1) only the date, (2) only the time, or (3) both the date and time.

To set the date/time format

1. Press Shift-F5 (Date/Outline).

2. Press 3 or F to choose Date Format. WordPerfect displays the Date Format menu.

3. Enter new options to format the date, the time, or both.

4. Press F7 (Exit) twice to return to your document.

The Date and Time options establish the format that WordPerfect uses to print the date and time. You can mix format numbers with any text that you want to print with the date and time; for example, your prompt may include the following: Today's date is: 3 1, 4, and the time is 8:9 0. With this prompt, WordPerfect enters the following when you use a Date/Time code or function: Today's date is March 19, 1990, and the time is 12:47 pm.

To print just the first three characters of month and day names, type a percent sign before the appropriate code. For example, typing %3. 1, 4 (%6) displays the following: Mar. 19, 1990 (Tue).

Deleting Text

WordPerfect's design permits you to delete unwanted text (from a single character to an entire page of characters) and insert additional text in several ways. Each approach works best in a specific situation.

Reminders

Remember to save your document using a name slightly different from that of the current version before you make major changes.

Keep in mind that the Del and Backspace keys are repeat keys. If you hold the key down (rather than press it once), Del or Backspace deletes multiple characters. The text to the right of the deleted characters moves in to fill the gap.

To delete a character at the cursor position

1. Use the arrow keys to position the cursor under the character to be deleted.

2. Press the Del key.

To delete a character to the left of the cursor

1. Move the cursor so that it is one character to the right of the character you want to delete.

2. Press the Backspace key. Doing so does not delete the character above the cursor. When you press the Backspace key, the character or code to the left of the cursor is erased. Any text to the right moves one character position to the left. Hold down the Backspace key to delete multiple characters to the left.

To delete a word at the cursor position

1. Position the cursor anywhere in the word to be deleted.

2. Hold down Ctrl while you press Backspace.

To delete a word to the left of the cursor

1. Place the cursor in the blank space to the right of the word to be deleted.

2. Hold down Ctrl while you press Backspace or press Home and then press Backspace.

To delete a word to the right of the cursor

1. Place the cursor on the first character of the word to be deleted.

2. Press Home and then press Del.

To delete a line of text

1. Position the cursor where you want to begin deleting text.

2. Press Ctrl-End (Delete to EOL [End of Line]).

To delete several lines at a time

1. Count the number of lines (following the cursor) you want to erase.

2. Press Esc. The message n=8 appears on the status line. The default repeat value number is 8, but you can change that number to reflect the number of lines to be deleted.

3. If the number is greater than or less than 8, type that number.

4. Press Ctrl-End (Delete to EOL).

To delete to the bottom of the current page

1. Position the cursor so that it is under the character that begins the page of text to be deleted. (Delete to EOP erases text that is between the cursor's position and the end of the current page.)

2. Press **Ctrl-PgDn** (**Delete to EOP** [End of Page]). The following prompt appears:

```
Delete Remainder of page? (Y/N)
No
```

3. Press **Y** to delete the text or press **N** if you have changed your mind.

To delete an entire page

1. Position the cursor anywhere on the page to be deleted.

2. Press **Ctrl-F4**.

3. Press **3** to select Page.

4. Press **3** to select Delete.

To delete blank lines

1. Move the cursor to the left margin at the beginning of the blank line.

2. Press **Del**. In some cases, a blank line may contain a return code ([HRt]) and a blank space that precedes the word at the start of the next line. You therefore may have to press Del more than once to delete the blank characters before you reach the hidden return code on that line.

To delete a block of text, refer to the section on Block commands.

Document Comments

You can insert nonprinting notes and reminders called *comments* into a WordPerfect document. You can display the comments on-screen, and you can convert the comments to text and print them. The Document Comments feature is useful for creating text for review by several authors.

To create a document comment

1. Press **Ctrl-F5** (**Text In/Out**) to display the following menu:

   ```
   1 DOS Text; 2 Password; 3 Save
   As; 4 Comment; 5 Spreadsheet: 0
   ```

2. Press **4** or **C** to choose Comment. WordPerfect displays the Document Comment menu:

   ```
   Comment: 1 Create; 2 Edit; 3
   Convert to Text: 0
   ```

3. Press **1** or **C** to choose Create. WordPerfect places the cursor in the Document Comment editing box.

4. Type the text of your comment in the comment box. Keep your text within the lines of the box— approximately seven lines of text. You may use bold or underline in the box.

5. Press **F7** (**Exit**) to return to the document.

The document comment appears in the middle of your text as a double-ruled box. The Comments Display option on the Setup: Edit Screen Options menu must be set to **Y**es.

If you want to print document comments, you must convert them to text.

To change a comment to text

1. Move the cursor to a point after the comment you want to convert.

2. Press **Ctrl-F5** (**Text In/Out**).

3. Press **4** or **C** to display the Comments menu.

4. Press **3** or **T** to choose Convert to Text.

WordPerfect searches backward from the cursor and converts the first comment found. (The comment is converted whether or not it is displayed.)

To change text to a comment

1. Press **Alt-F4** or **F12** (**Block**) and highlight the text.

2. Press **Ctrl-F5** (**Text In/Out**). WordPerfect prompts

   ```
   Create a comment? No (Yes)
   ```

3. Press **Y** to convert the marked text to a comment.

WordPerfect places the marked text inside a comment box.

You can choose whether to have WordPerfect display document comments on-screen.

To turn on and off comment display

1. Press **Shift-F1** (**Setup**) to display the Setup menu.

2. Press **2** or **D** to display the Display menu.

3. Press **6** or **E** to choose Edit Screen Options.

4. Press **2** or **C** to select Comments Display.

5. Press **Y** to display document comments in the text or press **N** to hide document comments.

6. Press **F7** (**Exit**) to return to your document.

Document Summary

You can create a document summary in which you keep the last revision date, the creation date, the document name and type, the author/typist name(s), the subject, an account (perhaps a customer name), keywords that you can search for from the List Files screen, and an abstract of up to 780 characters. You can type your own abstract or press **Shift-F10** (**Retrieve**) to use the first 400 characters from the document.

To turn on document summary for all documents

1. Press **Shift-F1** (**Setup**).

2. Press **3** or **E** to select Environment.

3. Press **4** or **D** to select Document Management/ Summary.

4. Press **1** or **C** to select Create Summary on Save/Exit and select **Y**es.

5. Press **F7** (**Exit**) to return to the editing screen.

To create a summary for one document or edit a summary

1. Press **Shift-F8** (**Format**).

2. Press **3** or **D** to select Document.

3. Press **5** or **S** to select Summary.

4. Complete the Document Summary screen to fit your needs.

Enhancing Text

You can change the size and appearance of your text to enhance your document. You can do some formatting as you enter text simply by pressing the appropriate key, typing the text, and pressing the key again. For example, both bold and underline are simple text enhancements that you can add as you type the text. You apply some text enhancements by selecting them from the Font menu—italic, for example.

Boldfacing Text

To create boldfaced text

1. Press **F6** (**Bold**).

2. Type the text. The text you type after pressing F6 appears brighter (or a different color) on-screen. The Pos number in the status line also changes in brightness or color.

3. Press F6 (Bold) again to turn off Bold.

Underlining Text

To create underlined text

1. Press F8 (Underline).

2. Type the text.

3. Press F8 (Underline) again to turn off Underline.

Changing the Base Font

WordPerfect's Font feature lets you choose among the fonts (typefaces) available for use with your printer and also controls size, color, and certain other variations of printed text, such as outline and shadow printing, subscripts and superscripts.

When you installed your printer, you selected the initial base font, the default base font, or the current font. (You can consider these terms interchangeable to avoid confusion.) The *base* font is the font in which text is normally printed. Other font sizes and appearance options are usually variations of the base font. If 10-point Helvetica is the base font, boldfaced text prints in 10-point Helvetica Bold, italics prints in 10-point Helvetica Italic, and so on.

The base font can be changed permanently or temporarily.

To change the base font

1. Move the cursor to the point in your document where you want to change the base font.

2. Press Ctrl-F8 (Font) to display the following Font menu:

```
1 Size; 2 Appearance; 3 Normal;
4 Base Font; 5 Print Color: 0
```

3. Press 4 or F to select Base Font. WordPerfect displays a list of the fonts available for use with your printer.

4. Use the cursor keys or Name Search feature to highlight the desired font.

5. Press 1 or S or Enter to select the font and return to your document.

The fonts listed are the printer's built-in fonts, plus any fonts you selected with the Cartridges and Fonts feature.

The screen display adjusts to reflect the number of characters that can be printed in a line with the new base font in the current margin settings. If you select a large font, for example, the on-screen lines are shorter than if you select a very small font, because with a large font fewer characters will fit on a line.

Changing Font Attributes

Font *attributes* refer to the variations in the current font's appearance. These variations are available with your printer for a given base font: size, italics, boldface, shadow printing, outline, small caps, and so on. Remember that how the variations appear depends on your printer.

To change font attributes

1. Press Ctrl-F8 (Font).

2. Press 1 or S to choose Size. The following menu appears:

```
1 Suprscpt; 2 Subscpt; 3 Fine;
4 Small; 5 Large; 6 Vry Large;
7 Ext Large: 0
```

Or press **2** or **A** to choose Appearance. The
following menu appears:

```
1 Bold; 2 Underln; 3 Dbl Und;
4 Italc; 5 Outln; 6 Shadw; 7 Sm
Cap; 8 Redln; 9 Stkout: 0
```

3. Press the number associated with the attribute of
   your choice.

You can change an attribute of existing text by first
blocking the text with **Alt-F4** or **F12** and then selecting
the new attribute as described in Steps 1–3.

To restore base fonts to normal after typing your text,
press **Alt-F3** or **F11** (**Reveal Codes**). Find the attribute
codes (they appear as paired codes). Press the right-
arrow key to move the cursor past the attribute off code.

When you have made a combination of attribute
changes, return the base font to normal by pressing
Ctrl-F8 (**Font**) and pressing **3** or **N** for Normal. This
selection cancels all size and appearance attributes.

Equations

WordPerfect includes a full-featured graphical-based
equation editor for creating mathematical equations. If
your printer can print graphics, WordPerfect graphically
prints your equations so that unusual symbols not
present in your printer's character set appear on the
page.

To create an equation

1. Press **Alt-F9** (**Graphics**).

2. Press **6** or **E** for Equation.

3. Press 1 or C for Create.

4. Press 9 or E for Edit.

You are now in WordPerfect's graphical equation editor. The top window displays the formula as it will be printed. You enter the formula in the bottom window. The right window displays a palette of mathematical commands, symbols, Greek characters, and other operators.

Type the formula—type A'='pi'times'r^2, for example—and press F9 to display the result. The ' character inserts a space into the equation. The space bar is used for separating commands only and does not put a space in the equation.

Press Shift-F3 (Switch) to move the cursor into the palette and then use the PgDn and arrow keys to cycle through special commands and symbols. The name of the character is displayed at the lower left of the screen, so you can simply type the name next time instead of moving into the palette.

Press Shift-F1 (Setup) to choose a font size if you want equations to appear larger than surrounding text.

Exiting to DOS

Even though WordPerfect's List Files feature can perform several common DOS functions, many times it is convenient to be able to "drop out" to DOS temporarily, perform operations, and then return to your document. Use Shell (Ctrl-F1) to exit to DOS.

Reminder

If you are running WordPerfect from the WordPerfect Library shell, invoking the Shell function returns you to the Library's Shell menu.

To exit to DOS temporarily with Shell

1. Press **Ctrl-F1** (**Shell**). WordPerfect prompts

   ```
   1 Go to Shell; Clipboard: 2 Save;
   3 Append; 4 Retrieve; 5 DOS
   Command: 0
   ```

2. Press **1** or **G** to go to the Shell menu. The asterisk displayed next to the WordPerfect menu choice indicates that the program is still active. You can run other programs depending on available memory.

3. To return to WordPerfect, press its menu choice letter (usually **W**).

To perform just one DOS command, press **5** or **C** for DOS Command.

To exit to DOS (not using Library Shell)

1. Press **Ctrl-F1**. WordPerfect prompts

   ```
   1 Go to DOS; 2 DOS Command: 0
   ```

2. Press the number next to the option you want to select.

Exiting WordPerfect

Reminder

If you exit WordPerfect incorrectly, you may lose the on-screen document and all the work that went into creating it. Exiting WordPerfect incorrectly generates an error message when you restart the program.

To exit WordPerfect

1. Press **F7** (**Exit**), and the following message appears:

```
Save Document? Yes (No)
```

The prompt provides you with one last opportunity to preserve your document before exiting WordPerfect. Be careful. If you do not save your document before you exit WordPerfect, you cannot retrieve the document later.

2. Press Y if you want to save your document or N if you do not want to save your document, type the file name under which you want to save the document, and then press Enter. The following message appears on-screen:

```
Exit WP? No (Yes)
```

3. Press Y to exit WordPerfect and return to DOS or press N to clear the screen and return to WordPerfect.

If you change your mind about exiting WordPerfect, press F1 (Cancel) to remain in WordPerfect and continue editing the current document.

When the DOS prompt or the Shell menu appears, you have exited WordPerfect. Now you can load another program or turn off your computer.

Files

With the List Files screen, you can perform standard DOS functions to manage your files. The options you can perform appear on the menu line of the List Files screen. For example, you can use this screen to copy, delete, rename, and move files. You can perform some operations on several files at a time by first *marking* the files.

Copying a File

To copy a file

1. Press **F5** (**List Files**).

2. Press **Enter** to view the list of files in the current directory. Or type the path of the directory you want to view and press **Enter**.

3. Move the highlight bar to the name of the document you want to copy. Or press **N** for Name Search, begin typing the name of the document, and press **Enter**.

4. Press **8** or **C** to choose Copy. The following prompt is displayed:

   ```
   Copy this file to:
   ```

5. Type the new destination and press **Enter**.

Deleting a File

To delete a file

1. Follow Steps 1–3 for copying a file.

2. Press **2** or **D** to choose Delete. The following prompt is displayed :

   ```
   Delete (filename)? No (Yes)
   ```

3. Press **Y** to delete the file.

Renaming or Moving a File

To rename or move a file

1. Follow Steps 1–3 for copying a file.

2. Press **3** or **M** to select Move/Rename. The following prompt appears, followed by the current name of the file:

New name:

3. Type the new name and press Enter.

If the file name you assign points to a directory other than the current subdirectory, WordPerfect moves the file. If you change only the file name without modifying the directory information, WordPerfect copies the file. If you change both, the file is moved using the new name.

Working with Several Files

You can mark several files with an asterisk and then delete, print, move, or copy the files in a single operation. Mark individual files by moving the highlight bar and then pressing the * key. Mark (or unmark) *all* files in the current subdirectory by pressing Home,*.

Find

WordPerfect 5 offers several useful ways to locate specific text. One of the most powerful tools is Word Search from the List (F5) menu. Greatly expanded from previous WordPerfect versions, Word Search searches through disk files for a given word or phrase that may be located on the first page, somewhere within the document, or in a document summary. Generally, you should try to limit a word search to only those files that meet special conditions.

Using the Word Search Command

To define Word Search conditions

1. Press F5 (List).

2. At the Dir prompt, enter a directory name to display all the files in a given directory.

3. Mark the files you want to include in the search by moving the cursor to the file name and pressing the asterisk (*) key. If you want to search all files, omit this step.

4. At the List Files screen, press 9 or F to choose Find. WordPerfect displays the Search menu:

   ```
   Find: 1 Name; 2 Doc Summary; 3
   First Pg; 4 Entire Doc; 5
   Conditions; 6 Undo: 0
   ```

5. To search only the document summaries of the marked files, press 1 or D to choose Doc Summary. WordPerfect prompts

   ```
   Word pattern:
   ```

6. Type a single word or a word pattern.

7. Press Enter to start the search.

   When the search is completed, the names of files in which the word pattern is located are displayed in a List Files screen marked with an asterisk. If no files contain the word pattern, a Not Found message is displayed and no files on the List Files screen are marked with asterisks.

   To move the cursor forward and backward from one marked file to another, use Tab and Shift-Tab, respectively.

8. To view a marked file, move the cursor to the file name on the List Files screen and then press 6 or L for Look. WordPerfect displays the text of the document whose name you have highlighted in the List Files screen.

9. To return to the List Files menu from the Word Search menu, keeping the same files marked after using Look, press F7 (Exit).

10. Press F7 (Exit) again to leave List Files. If you retrieve a file and want to return to the List Files screen with the same files still marked, select List Files twice.

To search only the first page of the marked files

1. Repeat Steps 1–4 in the preceding steps for defining Word Search conditions.

2. At the Search menu, press 3 or F to choose First Page.

3. Repeat Steps 6–10 in the preceding steps for defining Word Search conditions.

To search the entire text of each file you have marked

1. Repeat Steps 1–4 in the steps for defining Word Search conditions.

2. At the Search menu, press 4 or E to choose Entire Doc.

3. Repeat Steps 6–10 in the steps for defining Word Search conditions.

Using Wildcards To Search for Word Patterns

When you conduct a word search and WordPerfect prompts you to enter a word pattern (see Step 5 in the steps for defining Word Search conditions), you can use special wildcard characters. A question mark (?) represents a single character, and an asterisk (*) represents any number of characters up to a hard return. Here are some examples of allowable word patterns:

Pattern	Description
duck	WordPerfect finds files that contain the word *duck*.
d?ck	WordPerfect finds files that contain *duck*, *deck*, *Dick*, or *dock*.
d*k	WordPerfect finds files containing *duck*, *damask*, and *Derek*.
ducks can	WordPerfect finds files that contain such phrases as *ducks can waddle* and *ducks cannot stand on their heads*.
ducks*can	WordPerfect finds files that contain such text as *Ducks have adapted to many environments. They can.*
ducks,geese	WordPerfect finds files that contain either *ducks* or *geese*.
ducks;geese	WordPerfect finds files that contain both *ducks* and *geese*.

Upper- and lowercase letters are treated the same. In this respect, Word Search differs from WordPerfect's Search functions (F2 and Shift-F2), which match capitalized letters in a search string. If you enter Duck, Search does not stop at *duck*, but Word Search does mark files that contained either *duck* or *Duck*.

Footnotes and Endnotes

Footnotes and endnotes provide a simple, standard way of referencing sources as well as offering the reader additional parenthetical information.

Footnotes are inserted at the bottom or foot of the page; *endnotes* are grouped together at a location you specify, which is usually the end of your document or end of each chapter or section.

Both types of notes are marked in the text either by numbers or by special characters, such as asterisks (*). WordPerfect prints the footnote on the page with the text it references.

Creating Footnotes and Endnotes

To create a footnote or an endnote

1. Move the cursor to the position where you want to insert a footnote or endnote number.

2. Press Ctrl-F7 (Footnote) to display the Footnote/ Endnote menu.

3. Press 1 or F to display the Footnote menu or press 2 or E to display the Endnote menu.

4. Press 1 or C to select Create. An editing screen appears with the cursor to the immediate right of the current footnote or endnote number. You can use all the normal editing and function keys as you enter text. You can use spell-check within the note also.

5. Type the text.

6. Press F7 (Exit) to return to your document.

WordPerfect inserts a code that includes the first 50 characters of the note. You can view the code and partial text by pressing Alt-F3 or F11 for Reveal Codes. Press Shift-F7 and then 6 for View Document to display footnotes as they will appear when printed.

When a long footnote needs to be continued to the following page, WordPerfect leaves a half inch of the note of text on the first page. If not enough room is available to print a half-inch of the footnote and the line of text in which the footnote number occurs, both the text and footnote move to the next page.

Deleting Footnotes and Endnotes

Because the entire footnote (number and text) is in one code, you can delete the note in the same way you delete any other WordPerfect code.

To delete a footnote or endnote

1. Move the cursor under the footnote or endnote you want to delete.

2. Press Del.

3. Press Y to confirm the deletion.

WordPerfect renumbers the other notes in your document automatically.

Unlike footnotes, which are printed at the bottom of the page on which you create them, endnotes are placed together, at the end of the document or where you place an Endnote Placement code. Press Ctrl-F7 (Footnote) to position an Endnote Placement code.

Generating Endnotes

To generate endnotes

1. Press Alt-F5 (Mark Text).

2. Press 6 or G to choose Generate.

3. Press 5 or G to choose Generate Tables, Indexes, Cross References, etc. WordPerfect prompts

   ```
   Existing tables, lists, and
   indexes will be replaced.
   Continue? Yes (No)
   ```

4. Press Y to generate the endnotes.

The endnotes do not appear on-screen. Instead, WordPerfect replaces the message box with a new, boxed message:

```
Endnote Placement
```

If you want to use footnotes or endnotes but do not like the format WordPerfect has chosen for them, you can use Ctrl-F7 to change the numbering style, placement, and format.

Forms

WordPerfect documents are formatted for a particular size and type of paper. This formatting information is saved with the document in the form of a default Paper Size/Type specification or a special Paper Size/Type code that you enter in the document.

When you choose a form using the Paper Size/Type menu, WordPerfect displays the forms you designed, as well as the default form types supplied with the program. WordPerfect matches the forms from this Paper Type menu with the forms you define in the Form Type menu. If the program cannot find a corresponding definition, it chooses the form it considers to be the closest match.

WordPerfect comes with a list of default form sizes and types, and you also can add customized form definitions to meet your special needs.

You can change the following options when defining or editing a form type:

> *Form Size*
> *Form Type*
> *Font Type (portrait or landscape)*
> *Prompt to Load*
> *Location*
> *Double Sided Printing*
> *Binding Edge*
> *Labels*
> *Margin Offsets*

To select Paper Size/Type

1. Press Shift-F8 (Format).

2. Press 2 or P for Page.

3. Press 7 or S for Size of Paper.

4. Select one of the available options or create your own custom page size by pressing 2 or A for Add.

Function Keys

The keys labeled F1 to F10 on the left of the keyboard (or F1 to F12 at the top of the IBM Enhanced Keyboard) are *function keys*. Each function key can carry out four tasks when used by itself or in combination with another key.

The function keys are assigned as follows:

Function Key	*Name*
F1	Cancel
Ctrl-F1	Shell
Shift-F1	Setup
Alt-F1	Thesaurus
F2	→ Search
Ctrl-F2	Spell
Shift-F2	← Search
Alt-F2	Replace
F3	Help
Ctrl-F3	Screen
Shift-F3	Switch
Alt-F3 or F11	Reveal Codes
F4	→ Indent
Ctrl-F4	Move
Shift-F4	← Indent
Alt-F4 or F12	Block

F5	List
Ctrl-F5	Text In/Out
Shift-F5	Date/Outline
Alt-F5	Mark Text
F6	Bold
Ctrl-F6	Tab Align
Shift-F6	Center
Alt-F6	Flush Right
F7	Exit
Ctrl-F7	Footnote
Shift-F7	Print
Alt-F7	Columns/Table
F8	Underline
Ctrl-F8	Font
Shift-F8	Format
Alt-F8	Style
F9	End Field
Ctrl-F9	Merge/Sort
Shift-F9	Merge Codes
Alt-F9	Graphics
F10	Save
Ctrl-F10	Macro Define
Shift-F10	Retrieve
Alt-F10	Macro

Some function keys you use as toggle switches to turn a feature on and off. For example, to create boldface type, first press function key F6 (to turn on Bold); then type the text that will printed in boldface type and press F6 again to turn off Bold.

Some function keys permit you to select from a menu. Press Ctrl-F7, for example, and your system displays the Footnote/Endnote menu.

Some function keys start a feature that is ended when you press the Enter key. For example, activate the Center feature by pressing Shift-F6 and end centering by pressing Enter (or the ↓ key).

Graphics

With the Graphics feature, you can enhance the
appearance of your document with graphics boxes and
lines.

Defining Graphics Boxes

You can create five types of graphics boxes: figure, table
box, text box, user box, and equation. In these boxes,
you can insert text, graphic images, charts, or complex
mathematical equations with the equation editor. Or you
can create an empty box. Graphics boxes can be placed
in the body of a document, in headers, in footers, and in
endnotes. When you create a box, you specify its
contents, caption, type, placement on the page, and size.

To create a graphics box

1. Move the cursor to the point in your document
   where you want the box to appear.

2. Press **Alt-F9** (**Graphics**).

3. Select a box type.

   When you choose a box type, a menu appears.
   The name differs depending on the type of box
   you select; for example, if you select table,
   WordPerfect displays the following menu:

   ```
   Table Box: 1 Create; 2 Edit;
   3 New Number; 4 Options: 0
   ```

4. Press **1** or **C** to select Create.

   The Table: Definition menu appears. (Again, the
   name of the menu differs depending on the type of
   box you are creating.)

5. Select the options you want to specify.

6. Enter the changes.

7. Press F7 to return to your document.

For contents you can specify Graphic, which imports the graphic and makes it a permanent part of your WordPerfect document; Graphic on Disk, which saves disk space by not storing the image in your document; Text; or an equation you create with the equation editor.

Only an outline appears on-screen after you create a box. To see how the document will appear when printed, press Shift-F7 and then 6 for View Document.

Creating Graphics Lines

With WordPerfect, you can create vertical and horizontal lines on the printed page. The lines can be shaded or black, depending on your printer's capabilities.

To create graphics lines

1. Press Alt-F9 (Graphics).

2. Press 5 or L to select Line.

3. Press 1 or H to create a horizontal line or press 2 or V to create a vertical line. WordPerfect displays the Horizontal Line menu or the Vertical Line menu.

4. Choose an option and enter the appropriate information.

5. Press F7 (Exit) to return to the editing screen.

To edit a graphics line, position the cursor after the line code, press Alt-F9 (Graphics), and press 5 or L for Line; then press 3 or O to edit a horizontal line or press 4 or E to edit a vertical line.

Headers/Footers

A *header* is information (text, numbers, or graphics) that prints automatically at the margin at the top of pages. A *footer* is information printed automatically at the margin at the bottom of pages. Typical header and footer information may include chapter titles, page numbers, dates, and similar information.

To see headers or footers on-screen, either press Shift-F7 and then 6 for View Document or press Alt-F3 or F11 for Reveal Codes.

To create a header or footer

1. Press Shift-F8 (Format) to display the Format menu.

2. Press 2 or P to display the Format: Page menu.

3. Press 3 or H to select Headers or press 4 or F to select Footers. You can create two headers (A and B) and two footers (A and B). One of the following two prompts appears:

   ```
   1 Header A; 2 Header B: 0
   1 Footer A; 2 Footer B: 0
   ```

4. Press 1 or A, or 2 or B. WordPerfect displays the following menu:

   ```
   1 Discontinue; 2 Every Page; 3
   Odd Pages; 4 Even Pages; 5 Edit:
   0
   ```

5. Press 2 or P if you want the header (or footer) to appear on every page.

   Or press 3 or O if you want the header (or footer) to appear on odd pages only.

   Or press 4 or V if you want the header (or footer) to appear on even pages only.

6. Type the header (or footer) text using any of WordPerfect's formatting features.

7. Press F7 (Exit) twice to return to your document.

You can make changes to a header or footer from anywhere in a document. For example, you can change the text or the appearance of the text in your footer.

To make changes, select Edit from the Header or Footer menu. In addition to including and formatting text, you can add automatic page numbering to a header or footer by including ^B (Ctrl-B) in the header or footer. For example, you can specify the footer be numbered consecutively.

To include automatic page numbering in headers and footers

1. Type any text to precede the page number.

2. Press Ctrl-B.

3. Press F7 (Exit).

Help

WordPerfect has a context-sensitive on-line Help feature that you can access while working on WordPerfect documents. If you have a question about what a particular function key does, just press F3 (Help) to display information about that key. In addition to the function keys, the Help screens also explain the Esc, Del, Ins, Backspace, Tab, Home, and cursor-arrow keys. You can press F3 at any time.

To access Help

1. Press F3 (Help) to display the Help screen.

2. Press the key about which you want to know more.

For example, if you press Shift-F7 (Print), the Print Help menu is displayed. From within the Print Help screen, you can learn more about Printer Control by pressing 4 or C.

After you review the Help information, return to your file by pressing Enter or the space bar. If a menu was active when you pressed F3, leaving Help by pressing Enter or the space bar returns you to the menu.

Note

Press F3 (Help) twice to display the keyboard template. After accessing Help, type any letter of the alphabet to view a list of the features that begin with that letter.

Hyphenating Words

When a line of text becomes too long to fit within the margins, the last word wraps to the next line. With short words, wrapping doesn't present much of a problem. With long words, two problems can occur: (1) if justification is set to Left, large gaps can appear at the right margin, producing a document composed of very ragged text; (2) if justification is set to Full, large spaces between words become visually distracting.

Hyphenating the word at the end of the line solves these formatting problems. When you use WordPerfect's Hyphenation feature, the program fits as much of the word as possible on the line, hyphenates the word, and wraps the rest of the word to the next line.

Press Shift-F1 (Setup) to tell WordPerfect how to hyphenate words and press Shift-F8 (Format) to turn hyphenation on and off in your current document.

Configuring Hyphenation

1. Press **Shift-F1** (**Setup**) to display the Setup menu.

2. Press **3** or **E** to choose Environment.

3. Press **6** or **Y** for hyphenation.

4. Press **1** (**External Dictionary/Rules**) to hyphenate words according to the speller files or press **2** (**Internal Rules**) to have WordPerfect use a best-guess method.

5. Press **7** (**Prompt for Hyphenation**) to tell WordPerfect when it should ask for your help. Press **1** for Never, **2** for When Required, or **3** for Always.

This configuration is saved in the setup file WP{WP}.SET and is used for all documents.

Controlling Hyphenation within Individual Documents

To turn hyphenation on or off

1. Position the cursor at the point where you want to turn hyphenation on or off.

2. Press **Shift-F8** (**Format**).

3. Press **1** or **L** for Line.

4. Press **1** or **Y** for Hyphenation.

5. Press **Y** to turn on hyphenation or **N** to turn off hyphenation.

A [Hyph On] or [Hyph Off] code is inserted into your document.

If WordPerfect needs your help in hyphenating a word, the following prompt is displayed (followed by the word to be justified):

```
Position hyphen; Press ESC
```

To select hyphenation

Use the cursor keys to move the hyphen to another hyphenation point; then press Esc. Or press F1 (Cancel) if you don't want to hyphenate the word. If you don't hyphenate the word, it wraps to the next line and a Cancel Hyphenation code [/] is inserted before the word. You must delete the code manually if you later decide to hyphenate the word.

At first glance, a hyphen looks simply like a hyphen, but WordPerfect uses and permits you to use several kinds of hyphens.

A *hyphen character* is part of the spelling of a word, as in *father-in-law* and *jack-of-all-trades*. A hyphen character is displayed and printed at all times. The hyphen character code appears on the Reveal Codes screen as –. If a hyphen character appears in a word that needs to be hyphenated, WordPerfect uses the hyphen as the breaking point instead of prompting you for a hyphenation decision. To enter a hyphen character, simply press the Hyphen key (–), which is located on the same key as the underline character.

A *hard hyphen* appears the same on-screen as a hyphen character. WordPerfect treats a hard hyphen as if it were a character; the word containing a hard hyphen is not split at the hard hyphen when it falls within the hyphenation zone. On the Reveal Codes screen, the hyphen appears as an unhighlighted —. To enter a hard hyphen, press Home, Hyphen. Be sure to use the Hyphen key in the numeric key row, not the minus sign on the numeric keypad.

A *soft hyphen* is inserted between syllables during hyphenation. Soft hyphens are visible and print only when they appear as the last character in a line; otherwise, they remain hidden. A soft hyphen appears on the Reveal Codes screen as a highlighted —. You can insert soft hyphens at points where you want hyphenation to occur by pressing Ctrl-Hyphen.

A *deletable* soft return code [DSRt] is entered by WordPerfect when hyphenation is turned off and a long word extends from the left margin beyond the right margin. (The deletable soft return is not the same as the normal [SRt] soft return inserted at the end of a line by WordPerfect's word-wrap feature.)

The *invisible* soft return [ISRt] is useful for preventing empty spaces in lines caused by words separated by slashes, which WordPerfect normally treats as single, long words. To make expressions such as and/or or words connected with an ellipsis divide properly, press Home, Enter to insert an invisible soft return.

To insert a *dash* into your text, use a combination of two kinds of hyphens. For the first hyphen, press Home, Hyphen for the hyphen character. For the second hyphen, press the Hyphen key (–) for a hard hyphen. WordPerfect does not separate the two hyphens at the end of a line.

When you want to keep two or more words together—*San Francisco*, for example—insert a *hard space* between the words by pressing Home, space bar. Hard spaces signal WordPerfect to treat the words as a contiguous character string: WordPerfect does not divide the string when it falls at the end of a line but moves the entire word group to the following line.

Always press Alt-F3 or F11 for Reveal Codes when you want to delete unwanted hard and soft hyphens.

The Hyphenation Zone

WordPerfect decides which words to hyphenate by using a hyphenation zone. When hyphenation is on, the zone determines whether a word should be hyphenated or wrapped to the next line. The hyphenation zone is preset in percentages of line length: the left hyphenation zone is preset at 10%; the right hyphenation zone is set at 4%.

When hyphenation is turned on, three things can happen to words that fall near the right margin:

1. Words that start on or after the left hyphenation zone but do not reach the right margin remain in position.

2. Words that begin on or after the left hyphenation zone and pass the right margin wrap to the next line.

3. Words that start before the left hyphenation zone and pass over the right hyphenation zone require hyphenation.

The distance between the left and right hyphenation zones determines the size of words selected for hyphenation. The shorter the distance between the two zones, the more hyphenation is needed. You can use Shift-F8 (Format) to change the hyphenation zone temporarily.

Indenting

Although WordPerfect's Tab and Indent features are similar, they each have specific uses.

Tab	Indents only the first line of the paragraph from the left margin
F4	Indents the entire paragraph from the left margin
Shift-F4	Indents the entire paragraph from both the left and right margins

Press F4 (Indent) to indent an entire paragraph from the left margin. When you press F4, the cursor moves one tab stop to the right, and the left margin is reset temporarily. Everything you type, until you press Enter, is indented one tab stop. To indent more than one tab stop, press F4 until the cursor rests at the tab stop where you want to begin.

Press Shift-F4 (Left-Right Indent) to indent a paragraph from both the right and left margins. When you press Shift-F4, the cursor moves to the right one tab stop and temporarily resets both the left and right margins. Everything you type, until you press Enter, is indented one tab stop from the left margin and the same distance from the right margin. To indent more than one tab stop from both margins, press **Shift-F4** more than once.

To indent text from the left margin as you type

1. Move the cursor to the left margin.

2. Press F4 (Indent). The cursor moves to the next tab setting.

3. Type your text.

4. Press Enter to end indenting.

The text that you type now begins at the original left margin.

To indent text from both margins as you type

1. Press Shift-F4 (Left-Right Indent).

2. Type your text.

3. Press Enter to end indenting and return to the original margin settings.

To indent an existing paragraph

1. Move the cursor to the first character of the text you want to indent (or to the left of a tab indent at the beginning of a paragraph).

2. Press F4 (Indent) or Shift-F4 (Left-Right Indent).

3. Press ↓ to redraw the screen so that the entire paragraph is indented.

To create a hanging paragraph

A *hanging paragraph* is formed so that the first line is flush with the left margin and the rest of the paragraph is indented to the first tab stop.

1. Move the cursor to the left margin.

2. Press F4 (Indent) to move the cursor to the next tab stop.

3. Press Shift-Tab (Margin Release). The cursor moves back to its original position, at the left margin.

4. Type your text.

5. Press Enter to end the hanging paragraph.

Caution: Never use the space bar for indenting or tabbing. If your printer supports proportional spacing, text does not align properly at the left indent or tab stop. Instead, use the Tab or Indent key.

Indexing

WordPerfect's indexing feature creates an alphabetized list of index headings and subheadings (called *entries*) for a document. To create an index, press Alt-F5 (Mark Text) to *mark* or specify the words you want to include in the index, then define an index format, and finally generate the index.

You must place the index definition code at the end of your document; otherwise, the generated index omits marked text that comes after it.

Justifying Text

Use WordPerfect's Justification feature to align text on the left margin only, on the right margin only, on both margins (called *full* justification), or centered between the two margins.

To set justification

1. Press Shift-F8 (Format) to display the Format menu.

2. Press 1 or L to display the Format: Line menu.

3. Press 3 or J to select Justification.

4. Press 1 or L for Left Justification, 2 or C for Center, 3 or R for Right, or 4 or F for Full.

5. Press F7 (Exit) to return to your document.

Centering Text

With WordPerfect you can center text instantly. You can center a line (*horizontal centering*) as you type it or after you have entered it. You also can center a page from top to bottom (*vertical centering*).

To center text that you are about to type

1. Move the cursor to the left margin of the line you want to center.

2. Press Shift-F6 (Center). The cursor centers between the margins. As you type, the text adjusts to the left and to the right in order to stay centered.

   You can precede centered text with a row of dot leaders by pressing Shift-F6 (Center) twice.

3. Type your text and press Enter.

If you type more characters than can fit between the margins, the rest of the text moves to the next line. Only the first line is centered. To center several lines, use the Block Center function.

The preceding procedure works well for a single line of text. If you're typing more than one line of text, however, the best method is to do the following:

1. Press **Shift-F8**.

2. Press **L** to select Line.

3. Press **J** to select Justification.

4. Press **C** to select Center.

5. Type the text.

6. Repeat the procedure, but this time press **L** for Left rather than **C** for Center.

To center an existing line of text

1. Place the cursor at the left margin of the line of text you want to center.

2. Press **Shift-F6** (**Center**) to move the text to the center of the screen.

3. Press ↓.

The text appears centered on-screen. To center an existing line of text, the line must end with a hard return [HRt].

To center text around a specific point

1. With the cursor in the line to be centered, press **Alt-F3** or **F11** and make sure that no codes, characters, or spaces are on the line.

2. Press **Alt-F3** or **F11** again to leave the Reveal Codes screen.

3. Tab to the character position on which you want to center the text.

4. Press Shift-F6 (Center), type your text, and then press Enter.

The text is centered on the character position.

When you center a page top to bottom (*vertical centering*), the setting applies to just one page—the page where you make the setting. The end of a centered page can be defined either by a soft page break or by a hard page break. Ending the centered page with a hard page break ensures that it never accidentally merges with the next page. Usually a page centered top to bottom is a separate page and is shorter than the other pages in the document (like a title page).

To center text between the top and bottom margins

1. Place the cursor at the top left margin of the page.

2. Press Shift-F8 (Format) to display the Format menu.

3. Press 2 or P to display the Format: Page menu.

4. Press 1 or C for Center Page.

5. Press Y for Yes.

6. Press F7 (Exit) to return to your document.

Although the page does not move on-screen, it centers when you print your document. Use Reveal Codes to delete the [Center Pg] code.

When you insert the Center Top to Bottom code, be sure that the cursor rests at the beginning of the page before any other formatting codes. Press Alt-F3 or F11 (Reveal Codes) to verify the cursor position.

Flush Right

Flush Right (Alt-F6) aligns the right edge of all the headings, columns, and lines of text even (flush) with the right margin. You can make text align flush right either before or after you enter the text.

To create one line of flush-right text as you type

1. Press **Alt-F6** (**Flush Right**) to move the cursor to the right margin.

2. Type your text. As you type, the cursor stays at the right margin, and the text moves to the left.

3. Press **Enter** to end Flush Right.

Press **Alt-F6** (**Flush Right**) to align one line of text even (flush) with the right margin. Press **Shift-F8**, **L**, **J**, and **R** (**Right Justification**) to justify blocks of text on the right margin.

To right justify a block of existing text

1. Block the text to be right justified.

2. Press **Alt-F6** (**Flush Right**).

3. Press **Y** in response to the `[Just:Right]? No (Yes)` prompt.

WordPerfect inserts a `[Just:Right]` code before the block and another code after the block to restore the justification type previously in effect (Left, Center, or Full).

Line Spacing

To format your text, you can change both the line spacing and the line height.

WordPerfect's line-spacing default is single-spacing. To double-space or triple-space a document, you can change the line-spacing default instead of entering hard returns as you type. Line-spacing changes can be made permanently or temporarily. You will not see changes in line spacing on-screen except when you select single (1), double (2), or triple (3) line spacing.

To change line spacing temporarily

1. Press Shift-F8 (Format) to display the Format menu.

2. Press 1 or L to display the Format: Line menu.

3. Press 6 or S to select Line Spacing.

4. Type the amount of line spacing you want and press Enter. For example, to double-space, press 2. For 1 1/2 spaces, type 1.5 or 1 1/2.

5. Press F7 (Exit) to return to your document.

The vertical distance between the basline of text and the baseline of text above or below is called *line height*. WordPerfect automatically controls line height. If the line height was not adjusted and you changed to a larger type size, the vertical spacing would appear very cramped on the printed page.

Because WordPerfect handles line-height changes automatically, you usually don't need to adjust it manually except for special circumstances. If, for example, your document is one page plus two lines and you want the text to fit on one page, you can change the line height to accommodate the extra lines.

Use Shift-F8 (Format) to change line height.

Lists

If your document contains figures, illustrations, tables, and maps, you may want to list these resources in a reference table. Usually a list appears on a page by itself following the table of contents.

As with tables of contents, creating a list requires that you use Alt-F5 (Mark Text) to mark the text for the list, define the list, and generate the list.

You can create up to 10 lists per document. Lists 6 through 10 correspond to any captions you create for graphics figures, tables, text boxes, user boxes, and equations, respectively.

Locking Documents

You can *lock* your document so that no one (not even you) can retrieve or print it without the password. Other files associated with the document, such as backup files, undelete files, and move files, also are locked.

Reminder

If you forget a password, WordPerfect's technical support staff can do nothing to help. The document is unavailable forever.

To save your file as a locked document

1. Press Ctrl-F5 (Text In/Out).

2. Press 2 or P to select Password.

3. Press 1 or A to select Add/change.

4. Type the password and press Enter. The password can be up to 23 characters long. WordPerfect prompts

   ```
   Re-Enter Password:
   ```

5. Type the password again and press Enter.

Every time you retrieve or look at the document, WordPerfect asks you for the password. To unlock a document, follow Steps 1-2. For Step 3, press 2 or R to select Remove.

Long File Names

DOS file names are limited to 8 characters plus 3-character extensions. WordPerfect allows you to use descriptive file names of up to 68 characters, including spaces, and optional document types of up to 20 characters.

To activate long document naming

1. Press Shift-F1 (Setup).

2. Press 3 or E for Environment.

3. Press 4 or D for Document Management/Summary.

4. Press 3 or L for Long Document Names and respond Yes.

5. Optionally, press 4 or T to assign a default document type and enter up to 20 characters, such as memo, letter, report, or proposal.

6. Press F7 (Exit).

Whenever you save a document, WordPerfect prompts you for the long document name and document type. If the document is new, WordPerfect uses the long name and type to suggest a DOS file name that you can accept or edit before pressing Enter. Pressing F5 (List) causes the List Files display to show the long file name and type.

Macros

A macro is a file you create to represent a series of keystrokes. Macros automate time-consuming and tedious tasks such as typing Sincerely every time you write a business letter. After you set up a macro, you can use it to do almost instantly what would otherwise require many keystrokes.

Creating Macros

To record macro keystrokes

1. Press Ctrl-F10 (Macro Define) to turn on the macro definition recorder. The following prompt appears in the lower left corner of your screen:

   ```
   Define macro:
   ```

   This prompt is asking for the name of your macro. WordPerfect has three ways to name a macro when the Define Macro: prompt is displayed:

Alt-*letter*	Press and hold the Alt key as you type a letter between A and Z. Use Alt-*letter* names for macros you want to save and use again.
Enter macro	Creates a temporary macro you will use only until you create another temporary macro, do not type a name; just press Enter. WordPerfect names the macro.
Named macro	Type a descriptive one- to eight-character name and press Enter. Named macros can be used over and over.

2. Type the macro name and press Enter; or, for a temporary macro, just press Enter. WordPerfect prompts

   ```
   Description:
   ```

3. Enter a description of up to 39 characters that tells what the macro does. For a temporary macro, skip this step. WordPerfect does not prompt you to enter a description.

4. Press Enter to begin recording keystrokes. For a temporary macro, skip this step.

   The Macro Def prompt blinks in the lower left of the screen. Think of this blinking message as a reminder that the program is recording and remembering your keystrokes.

5. Type the keystrokes (function keys and/or text) that you want to record in the macro file. Type the keystrokes in the exact order that you want them played back when you run the macro.

6. Press Ctrl-F10 (Macro Define) to end macro definition.

WordPerfect now saves the macro in a permanent disk file in the subdirectory you specified in Setup, Location of Files and returns you to the document screen.

Running Macros

The way you run (play back) a macro depends on the method you used to name the macro.

Reminder

Keep in mind that you can stop a macro while it is running by pressing F1 (Cancel). A macro stops automatically if it encounters an error message or if it contains a Search or Replace function and cannot locate the search text.

To run an Alt-letter macro

Press and hold down the Alt key while you type the
letter assigned to the macro—for example, Alt-B.

To run a named macro

1. Press Alt-F10 (Macro).

2. Type the name of the macro you want to run.

3. Press Enter.

To run a temporary Enter-key macro

1. Press Alt-F10 (Macro).

2. Press Enter.

Margins, Left and Right

WordPerfect presets all initial or default settings for
margins, tabs, and other basic features. If these settings
do not fit your needs, you can change the settings
(temporarily) for the document on which you are
working, or you can change the settings permanently by
pressing Shift-F1 for the Setup menu.

WordPerfect's default margins are 1 inch for the left and
1 inch for the right—appropriate margins for 8 1/2-by-
11-inch paper. WordPerfect 5.1 measures margins from
the right and left edges of the paper, or from the
perforation for pin-feed paper.

If you want to change the margins, simply measure your
stationery or paper and decide how many inches of
white space you want as margins. Because measuring in
rows and columns can be confusing, set margins in
inches.

New margin settings override previous settings. You can change margins in the middle of a line, but WordPerfect will enter a hard return [HRt] before the new margin code to ensure that the current line is formatted with the existing margins and that text that follows the code is formatted with the new margins.

To change the left and right margin settings

1. Place the cursor at the left margin of the line where you want the new margin setting to begin.

2. Press Shift-F8 (Format) to display the Format menu.

3. Press 1 or L to display the Format: Line menu.

If you change your mind about the new margin settings, pressing F1 (Cancel) will not cancel the new settings; you must press Alt-F3 or F11 for Reveal Codes to remove the [L/R Mar:1",1"] code.

If you always use different margins than the default, you can permanently change the margins for all future documents.

To change the left and right margins permanently

1. Press Shift-F1 (Setup).

2. Press 4 or I to display the Initial Settings menu.

3. Press 5 or C for Initial Codes.

4. Press Shift-F8 (Format).

5. Press 1 or L to display the Format: Line menu.

6. Press 7 or M to select Margins (Left/Right).

7. Type a new value for the left margin and press Enter.

8. Type a new value for the right margin and press
   Enter.

9. Press F7 (Exit) three times to return to your
   document.

Margins, Top and Bottom

To change the top and bottom margins

1. Move the cursor to the position in your document
   where you want to set margins—usually at the
   beginning of the document.

2. Press Shift-F8 (Format) to display the Format
   menu.

3. Press 2 or P to display the Format: Page menu.

4. Press 5 or M to select Margins (Top/Bottom).

5. Type a new top margin in decimal inches and
   press Enter. If, for example, you want a top
   margin of 1 1/2 inches, type 1.5 and press Enter.

6. Type a new bottom margin in decimal inches and
   press Enter.

7. Press F7 (Exit) to return to your document.

You can use WordPerfect's Advance feature to insert
into your document a code that instructs your printer to
move left, right, up, or down before printing. You also
can use Advance to tell your printer to start printing at a
specific location on the page. (Some printers cannot
"advance" backward.) Advance provides a way to move
text down on the page to compensate for letterheads and
logos on starting pages.

Master Documents

A master document file consists of two kinds of files: master document files and subdocument files. The master document file is a regular WordPerfect file that contains codes that reference the subdocument files. In addition to the codes, the master document file can contain anything else you want to include (like the table of contents). The subdocument contains the text for each section of the total document. You can include as many subdocuments as you need.

A subdocument can also have subdocuments of its own.

To use Master Document to manage large projects

1. Maintain and store sections of a long document as individual files called *subdocuments*.

2. Build a skeleton or *master document* that includes references to each subdocument.

3. Temporarily *expand* the master document to link all the individual files (to generate a table of contents, for example).

4. Separate or *condense* the expanded document into its component parts (subdocuments).

Math

WordPerfect's Math feature is designed to provide limited calculation capabilities for simple math operations, like preparing an invoice or developing a sales report.

Vertical Column Calculation

WordPerfect allows you to calculate and display the totals of numbers in columns.

To calculate in vertical columns

1. Set the tabs for your columns.

2. Define the type and format of your columns.

3. Turn on Math, using **Alt-F7** (**Math/Columns**).

4. Enter caption text, numbers, and math operators in the columns.

5. Calculate the results.

6. Turn off Math.

You enter both the numbers for your columns and math operators to perform calculations. You can use as many as six Math operators in a Math numeric column, as shown in the following table.

WordPerfect Math Operators

Hier. Level	*Operator*	*Function*
2	+ (Subtotal)	Adds all numbers in the column above the + sign (from the last total or subtotal taken or from the beginning of the column).
2	t (Extra Subtotal)	Treats the number immediately following this operator as a subtotal.
3	= (Total)	Adds all subtotals (+) and extra subtotals (t) since the last total.

3	T (Extra Total)	Treats the number immediately following this operator as a total.
4	* (Grand Total)	Adds all totals (=) and extra totals (T) since the last grand total.
1, 2, 3	N (Negate)	Reverses the sign of the result or number immediately following this operator for use in further calculations.

Math operators are symbols that tell WordPerfect both the type of calculation you want to perform and where the result will be displayed. You enter a Math operator by using the Tab key to position the cursor at the location where the results should be displayed and then entering the appropriate operator.

When you enter an operator, only the operator is displayed (the math results are not shown until you invoke the Calculate function).

Horizontal Calculations

Numeric and total columns calculate vertical addition of numbers. You can use Alt-F7 (Columns/Table) to calculate another type of Math column—the calculation (0) column. Calculation columns calculate numbers within the same line of a WordPerfect document and are also called horizontal calculations.

When you enter 0 for the column type code, WordPerfect automatically moves the cursor down to the middle of the screen to allow you to enter a formula for the calculation column.

Formulas are composed of numbers, column identifiers, and math operators. *Do not use spaces in calculation formulas*. Your formulas can include the following four standard arithmetic operators:

+ Add

- Subtract

* Multiply

/ Divide

The formula is calculated from left to right. If you want a math term to calculate before other items, enclose that term in parentheses. Unlike algebra, however, you *cannot* use nested parentheses, as in (3+(3*A))-B. If you want to use a fraction in an equation, place it in parentheses or use its decimal equivalent: (1/3) or .33 .

You may find that using the Tables feature gives you more control over math.

Merge

Merge inserts variable data into a fixed format. With WordPerfect's Merge feature, you can create personalized form letters from an address list, produce phone lists, print labels, piece together complicated reports, or fill in forms.

Assembling Documents with Merge

WordPerfect uses just two documents to perform a merge.

The *primary (document) file* holds a skeleton document into which pieces of data are merged. Most of the primary file remains constant. The primary file contains two elements: the fixed text and the merge codes, which are implanted where the variable items will be added to the fixed text.

The *secondary (data) file* contains the data, or variable information, that is merged into the primary file. Information in the secondary file is organized like information on filing cards. The information on one filing card (or one secondary file entry) is known as a *record*. Records are divided into *fields*. For example, mailing list fields usually consist of the first name, last name, company name, street address, city, state, and ZIP code.

Creating the secondary file—the data file—is usually the first step in the merge procedure.

Reminders

Remember that a secondary file consists of records (ending with {END RECORD}), which have a number of fields (ending with {END FIELD}). The structure must be uniform; otherwise, the merge will not work properly.

Keep in mind that every data record must have the same number of fields.

The fields in all records must be in the same order. For example, if the first name is in field 1, but one record has the last name in field 1, WordPerfect will print a last name where the first name should be.

To create a sample secondary file

1. Clear the screen and place the cursor at the top left margin.

2. Type a name and address, pressing F9 (End Field) at the end of the each line (field). When you press F9, WordPerfect inserts an {END FIELD} code and a hard return [HRt] code.

3. At the end of the last line of the record, press Shift-F9 (Merge Codes) after you press F9 (End Field).

4. Press 2 or E to enter an {END RECORD} code that marks the end of the record. WordPerfect enters an {END RECORD} code and a hidden Hard Page [HPg] code.

5. Enter the next record.

6. When you finish entering data, save the file under a name that indicates its purpose: LETTERS.DAT or NAMES.MRG, for example.

Creating Primary Files

A primary file contains fixed text and special merge codes. The codes guide WordPerfect to bring in specific records from your secondary merge file and these records where the codes are implanted. The most common code is the field number code {FIELD}n^. The n indicates a field number (or name) of each record in the secondary file.

To create a sample primary file

1. Begin typing a sample letter. When you get to the line where you want the addressee's name entered, press Shift-F9 (Merge Codes). WordPerfect displays the Merge Codes menu:

```
1 Field; 2 End Record; 3 Input;
4 Page Off; 5 Next Record; 6
More: 0
```

2. Press F. WordPerfect prompts

```
Field:
```

3. Press the number of the current field (1, in this case) and then press Enter, because you want field 1 (name, for example) from the secondary file to be printed here. WordPerfect inserts a {FIELD}1~ code into your document at the cursor.

4. Repeat Steps 1–3 for field 2 (company), field 3 (address), field 4 (city), and field 5 (salutation).

5. When you finish typing the letter, save it with a name that indicates its purpose: LETTER.MRG or MERGE.LET, for example.

Your primary file will now show the information merged from the secondary file.

Running a Merge

The codes {FIELD}1~, {FIELD}2~, {FIELD}3~, and so on, instruct WordPerfect to reach into the secondary (data) file, copy the appropriate fields, and insert them into the letter. For example, WordPerfect inserts field 1 at {FIELD}1~, field 2 at {FIELD}2~, and so on.

To merge primary and secondary files

1. Press Ctrl-F9 (Merge/Sort). WordPerfect displays the Merge/Sort menu:

   ```
   1 Merge; 2 Sort; 3 Convert Old
   Merge Codes: 0
   ```

2. Press 1 or M to select Merge. WordPerfect prompts

   ```
   Primary file:
   ```

3. Type the name of the primary (document) file in which you saved the letter and then press Enter. Or press F5 (List) to highlight a file and select Retrieve. WordPerfect prompts

   ```
   Secondary file:
   ```

4. Type the name of the secondary (data) file in which you saved the address data and then press Enter. Or press F5 as in the preceding step.

The two files are merged, and the resulting merge-printed letters are displayed on the screen. You can edit them now or save them in a file.

To merge directly to the printer

1. At the end of the primary file (the text of the letter), press **Shift-F9** (**Merge Codes**) and then press **6** or **M** for More. A box appears listing advanced merge programming commands.

2. Press **P** to advance to the first command beginning with P. Scroll down until the {PRINT} command is highlighted.

3. Press **Enter** to insert the {PRINT} code into your primary file.

4. Repeat steps 1 and 2 and then press **Enter** to insert the {NEXT RECORD} code.

5. Repeat steps 1 and 2 to select {NEST PRIMARY} and press **Enter** twice to insert {NEST PRIMARY}~ into your document.

   {PRINT} sends to the printer all text merged so far.

   {NEXT RECORD} moves to the next name and address record in the secondary file.

   {NEST PRIMARY}~ starts the merge again, using the same primary file.

6. Save the letter.

7. Turn on the printer.

8. Press **Ctrl-F9** (**Merge/Sort**) to start the merge operation.

9. Press **1** or **M** to choose Merge.

10. Type the primary file name and press **Enter**.

11. Type the secondary file name and press **Enter**.

WordPerfect prints your letters.

Creating Labels

You can use Merge to print labels on various kinds of label stock.

Reminder

First create a secondary (name and address) file. Then you can use that file to print mailing labels.

To create the primary file for labels

You must create a form for the label stock you plan to use. You can use the LABELS macro or manually define a new form:

1. Press Alt-F10 (Macro) and type LABELS to run the LABELS macro supplied with WordPerfect. Select one label size by moving the highlight bar and pressing Enter or select several labels by marking them with an * and then pressing Enter. Each label you select is added to your list of forms.

   To create a label form manually (or if the labels you have are not listed in the LABELS macro), press Shift-F8 (Format). Press 2 or P for Paper Size/ Type, 7 or S for Paper Size, 2 or A for Add, 4 or L for Labels, 8 or A for Labels, and Y for Yes. Then enter all appropriate dimensions and location information.

   After a label form is defined, you don't need to repeat this step.

2. With a clear screen, build your primary file by selecting the appropriate label form from the Paper Size/Type menu.

3 Continue by entering {FIELD} codes from the Merge Codes menu corresponding to the fields in your secondary file.

4. Save the primary file and then press Ctrl-F9 to begin the merge.

Mouse

Before using a mouse, you must first configure
WordPerfect (see "Customizing WordPerfect").

You can use a mouse to move the cursor, block text, and
make selections from menus that "pull down" from the
top of the screen. WordPerfect's mouse implementation
is not intended to make you think you have a Macintosh.
The functions provided are rudimentary by design.

To move the cursor with the mouse

1. Manipulate the mouse to move its rectangular
   pointer on the screen.

2. Click the left button once.

You can scroll the document by holding down the right
button and dragging the mouse pointer to any screen
edge. Release the button to stop the scrolling.

To block text with the mouse

1. Move the mouse pointer to either end of the block.

2. Press and hold down the left button while dragging
   the pointer to the opposite end of the block.

3. Release the left button.

To use the pull-down menus

1. Click the right button to display the menu bar.

2. Move the pointer to a menu choice and click the left
   button to display a pull-down menu. Items with
   triangles pointing to the right have additional
   submenus.

3. Continue to click with the left button or hold down
   the button and drag the mouse to make choices.

Pressing the right button is the same as pressing F1 (Cancel). Displayed menus disappear, and choices already made are canceled.

You can use the pull-down menus without a mouse. Use the Setup: Menu Options screen to set your program so that the menus are displayed when you press Alt key combinations.

Numbering Lines

With line numbering, you can easily refer to a particular clause in a legal document or to a specific passage in a manuscript. For example, you can refer to page 11, line 26 to cite a passage.

When you begin Line Numbering, WordPerfect inserts a [Ln Num:On] code in your document and begins numbering that line at 1. Numbers are not displayed on-screen; they appear when you print the document or when you press Shift-F7 and then 6 for View Document.

To turn on line numbering

1. Move the cursor to the position where you want line numbering to begin.

2. Press Shift-F8 (Format).

3. Press 1 or L to display the Format: Line menu.

4. Press 5 or N to select Line Numbering.

5. Press Y to turn on Line Numbering and display the Format: Line Numbering menu.

6. Press Enter to accept the default settings. Or select the option you want to change, enter the desired information, and then press F7 (Exit).

To turn off Line Numbering, repeat Steps 1–4.
For Step 5, press N.

Numbering Pages

Automatic page numbering is as easy as telling
WordPerfect how and where you want the numbers to
appear on the page. Numbering begins with whatever
number you select. Be sure to place the cursor at the
beginning of your document if you want page
numbering to begin on the first page.

You can select any one of three basic page number
positions: (1) top of the page (left, right, or center), (2)
bottom of the page (left, right, or center), or (3) facing
pages (at the left side of even pages or at the right side
of odd pages).

To select page number position

1. Press Shift-F8 (Format) to see the Format menu.

2. Press 2 or P to display the Format: Page menu.

3. Press 6 or N to display the Format: Page
   Numbering menu. You can enter information for
   the following items.

   New Page Number. Enter the number with which
   you want numbering to begin. You may want to
   assign 1 to the first page of a report even though it
   comes after the title page and table of contents.
   (You can enter Roman numerals here, if desired.

   Page Number Style. Enter any punctuation you
   want, such as -^B- or Page ^B.

   Insert Page Number. Insert the page number at the
   cursor location on the current page only.

Page Number Position. Position page numbers at the top of the page (left, right, or center), at the bottom of the page (left, right, or center), or on facing pages (left top or bottom of even pages and right top or bottom of odd pages).

4. Type the number that corresponds to the position where you want page numbers to appear.

5. Press F7 (Exit) to return to your document.

To delete page numbering

1. Move to the position where you invoked the page numbering function.

2. Press Alt-F3 or F11 (Reveal Codes).

3. Delete the [Pg Numbering:] code.

To turn off page numbering

You can turn off page numbering for the entire document or for a section of the document.

1. Move the cursor to the point where you want to discontinue page numbering.

2. Press Shift-F8 (Format) to see the Format menu.

3. Press 2 or P to display the Format: Page menu.

4. Press 6 or P for Page Numbering.

5. Press 4 or P for Page Number Position.

6. Press 9 or N for No Page Numbers.

7. Press F7 (Exit) to return to your document.

To suppress page numbering for a single page

You can suppress page numbering for a single page. For example, you may not want the title page of a report to have a page number.

1. Move to the top of the page on which you want numbering suppressed.

2. Press Shift-F8 (Format) to see the Format menu.

3. Press 2 or P to display the Format: Page menu.

4. Press 8 or U to select Suppress (this page only).

5. Press 4 or P to select Suppress Page Numbering.

6. Press Y.

7. Press F7 (Exit) twice to return to your document.

Numbering Paragraphs

Paragraph Numbering differs from Outline because you must insert numbers manually. But, unlike Outline, Paragraph Numbering lets you choose the level number, regardless of the cursor position. Paragraph Numbering may be easier to edit if, for example, your document has few outline numbers and a great deal of text.

You can select a numbering style for Paragraph Numbering.

To number paragraphs

1. Move the cursor to the left margin of the paragraph you want to number.

2. Press Shift-F5 (Date/Outline).

3. Press 5 or P to choose Para Num. WordPerfect prompts

   ```
   Paragraph Level (Press Enter for
   Automatic):
   ```

4. Type the level number you want to assign and press Enter, or just press Enter. If you press Enter for automatic numbering, the number or letter that WordPerfect inserts corresponds to the cursor

position. With the cursor at the left margin, WordPerfect inserts a level 1 number; with the cursor at the first tab stop, WordPerfect inserts a level 2 number, and so on.

5. Complete Steps 1–4 for each of the paragraphs you want to number.

WordPerfect's default numbering style is for outlines. To select a style more appropriate for numbering paragraphs, press Shift-F5 and press 6 or D for Define.

Outlines

WordPerfect's Outline feature permits you to create an outline and generate paragraph numbers automatically. Outlines in WordPerfect are simply normal text with a [Par Num] code inserted where each paragraph number appears in the printed document. Each time you press Enter, you create a new paragraph number. Within the line, each time you press Tab, you create a different level number.

The style you select determines the characters used for each level. The default paragraph numbering style is Outline (uppercase Roman numerals for level 1, uppercase letters for level 2, Arabic numbers for level 3, and so on).

To create an outline

1. If you want to title your outline, press Shift-F6 (Center), type the title, and press Enter.

2. Move the cursor to the position on the page where you want the outline to begin.

3. Press Shift-F5 (Date/Outline). The following menu appears:

```
1 Date Text; 2 Date Code; 3 Date
Format; 4 Outline; 5 Para Num; 6
Define: 0
```

4. Press **4** or **O** to turn on Outline.

5. Press **1** or **O** for On.

6. Press **Enter** to insert the first paragraph number in the outline (*I.* in Outline style).

7. To place the number and move the cursor, press **F4** (**Indent**).

8. Type the text for the first entry.

9. Press **Enter** to move to the next line and automatically enter the next number. Press **Enter** again to insert a blank line, if you want (the number moves down with the cursor).

10. WordPerfect by default indents automatically to the same level as the preceding entry. Press **Tab** to move in an additional level or press **Shift-Tab** to move out one level..

11. To place the number and move the cursor, press **F4** (**Indent**).

12. Type the text for this entry and press **Enter**.

13. Follow Steps 5–11 to complete your outline.

If you press **Tab** too many times, you can move back a level by pressing **Shift-Tab** (**Margin Release**).

To turn off the outline feature

1. Press **Shift-F5** (**Date/Outline**).

2. Press **4** or **O** to choose Outline.

To change the numbering style

1. Move the cursor to a location before the beginning of the outline.

2. Press **Shift-F5** (Date/Outline).

3. Press **6** or **D** to choose Define.

4. Choose from the selection of predefined numbering styles (2 through 5 on the menu).

5. Press **8** or **A** if you do not want the cursor to indent the preceding entry's level automatically.

6. Press **F7** (Exit) twice to return to your document.

With the Styles feature, you can create a special outline style that automatically formats each level of your outline with bold, underline, font, or other codes.

Page Breaks

WordPerfect offers you several options for controlling page breaks. WordPerfect's automatic page breaks are based on one-inch top and bottom margins. The actual number of text lines that fit is affected by the font size, line height, line spacing, and presence of headers, footers, footnotes, or page numbering.

WordPerfect inserts a dashed line in your document on-screen wherever an automatic page break occurs. These *soft page breaks* produce a hidden [SPg] code. When you add or delete text from a page, soft page breaks are recalculated automatically.

To force a page break at a certain spot, enter a *hard page break*. The page always ends at that point. On-screen a hard page break appears as a double-dashed line. On the Reveal Codes screen (Alt-F3 or F11), a hard page break is displayed as [HPg].

You also can control where a page breaks with the Conditional End of Page function, the Block Protect command, and the Widows and Orphans feature.

To insert a hard page break

1. Move the cursor to the beginning of the text that should appear on a new page.

2. Press **Ctrl-Enter**.

To delete a hard page break

Move the cursor to the beginning of the line just below the double-dashed line and press **Backspace**.

Or move the cursor to the last space before the double-dashed line and press **Del**.

Or press **Alt-F3** or **F11** (**Reveal Codes**), delete the [Hpg] code, and press **Alt-F3** or **F11** (**Reveal Codes**).

If you insert text into a page that ends with a hard page break, the hard page break may move beyond the point at which WordPerfect normally inserts a soft page break, creating an extra page that has only a few lines.

To use the Conditional End of Page command

1. Count the lines that must remain together on the same page.

2. Move the cursor to the line above the lines you want to keep together.

3. Press **Shift-F8** (**Format**) to see the Format menu.

4. Press **4** or **O** to display the Format: Other menu.

5. Press **2** or **C** for Conditional End of Page. WordPerfect prompts

   ```
   Number of Lines to Keep Together:
   ```

6. Type the number of lines you counted in Step 1 and press **Enter**.

7. Press **F7** (**Exit**) to return to your document.

The Conditional End of Page command groups a given number of lines so that they do not break across two pages. Use this command, for example, when you want to be sure that the title in a document is followed by at least three lines of text.

To use the Block Protect command

1. Press Alt-F4 or F12 (Block).

2. Highlight the text you want to protect. When you define the block, move the cursor to the end of the block but don't include the final return at the end of a paragraph.

3. Press Shift-F8 (Format). WordPerfect displays the following prompt:

   ```
   Protect block? No (Yes)
   ```

4. Press Y to protect the block.

Notes

Block Protect is similar to Conditional End of Page, but instead of specifying a number of lines, you define the text you want to protect as a block. If you later add or subtract lines from the block, WordPerfect keeps the block on the same page.

WordPerfect can automatically prevent single lines from being "stranded" at the top or bottom of a page. The first line of a paragraph left at the bottom of a page is called a *widow*; the last line of a paragraph left at the top of a page is called an *orphan*. Activating the Widow/Orphan Protection at the beginning of your document prevents their occurrence throughout the entire document.

To invoke widow/orphan protection

1. Position the cursor where you want the protection to begin.

2. Press Shift-F8 (Format) to see the Format menu.

3. Press 1 or L to display the Format: Line menu.

4. Press 9 or W to select Widow/Orphan Protection.

5. Press Y to turn on Widow/Orphan Protection.

6. Press F7 (Exit) to return to your document.

Widow/Orphan Protection remains in effect until you turn it off.

Paragraph Spacing

When you finish a paragraph, you usually press Enter twice to insert a blank line. Alternatively, you can press Enter just once at the end of a paragraph and have WordPerfect insert extra spacing for you. This procedure is called *adding leading*.

To increase the height of a hard return

1. Press Shift-F8 (Format).

2. Press 4 or O for Other.

3. Press 6 or P for Printer Functions.

4. Press 6 or L for Leading Adjustment.

5. Press Enter to move the cursor to Secondary.

6. Type 1u and press Enter.

7. Press F7 (Exit) to return to the editing screen.

Entering 1u tells WordPerfect to add one extra line space based on the current line height. The *u* is actually WordPerfect's way of specifying old-style WordPerfect 4.2 units of measurement that were expressed as lines.

Positioning Text

You control where text prints on the page by selecting the paper size, setting top and bottom margins, and using the Advance feature.

WordPerfect assumes that you use 8 1/2-by-11-inch paper. If you want to use legal-size paper (8 1/2-by-14-inches), you can change the paper size. You can choose predefined paper sizes, or you can define your own size.

To change paper size and type

1. Press Shift-F8 (Format) to display the Format menu.

2. Press 2 or P to display the Format: Page menu.

3. Press 7 or S to select Paper Size/Type. WordPerfect displays the Format: Paper Size menu.

4. Choose a paper type from the predefined types listed.

5. Press F7 (Exit) to return to your document.

WordPerfect is preset to leave one-inch margins at the top and bottom of the page. Page numbers, headers, footers, and footnotes must fit within this text area.

To use Advance

1. Position the cursor at the location where you want Advance to begin.

2. Press Shift-F8 (Format) to see the Format menu.

3. Press 4 or O to display the Format: Other menu.

4. Press 1 or A to choose Advance. You can advance up, down, right, left, or to a specified position.

5. Type the number associated with your selection.

6. Type the distance to advance and press Enter. The
    distance you enter is relative to the current cursor
    position. If you choose Line, the number you enter
    is the distance down from the top edge of the page.
    If you choose Position, the number you enter is the
    distance in from the left edge of the page.

7. Press F7 (Exit) to return to your document.

To return the print head to its original position, enter a
separate code to advance in the opposite direction.

Preview Document

Use the View Document feature to view your document
before printing. You will save costly printer paper and
time by first previewing your document. Document
pages appear on-screen as they will appear when printed
on paper, including graphics (if your system can display
graphics), footnotes, page numbers, line numbers,
headers, footers, and justification.

To preview your document

1. Position the cursor where you want to view.

2. Press Shift-F7 (Print).

3. Press 6 or V to view the document.

4. Press 1 (100%) to view the document at its actual
    size, 2 (200%) to view the document at twice its
    actual size, 3 (Full Page) to view the entire page, or
    4 (Facing Pages) to view the current page and its
    facing page (odd-numbered pages are displayed on
    the right side of the screen, and even-numbered
    pages are displayed on the left).

5. Press PgUp or PgDn or Ctrl-Home (GoTo) to
    view other pages of the document.

6. Press F7 (Exit) to return to your document.

Print Cartridges & Fonts

The Cartridges and Fonts feature on the Printer Settings menu lists the fonts that WordPerfect can use with your printer. You can mark the fonts you plan to use; these fonts appear on the Base Font and Initial Font menus.

To install cartridges and fonts

1. Press Shift-F7 (Print).

2. Press S to choose Select Printer.

3. Use the cursor keys to highlight the name of the printer you want to edit.

4. Press 3 or E to choose Edit.

5. If prompted to insert a printer disk, do so and type the drive letter.

6. Press 4 or C to choose Cartridges and Fonts. WordPerfect displays the Select Printer: Cartridges and Fonts menu. If you cannot remember which disk contains your printer definition, insert each Printer disk and press 4 or C until the menu appears.

7. Move the cursor to a font category.

8. Press 1 or F to choose Select Fonts. WordPerfect displays another Select Printer: Cartridges and Fonts menu.

9. Move the cursor to a cartridge or font you want to use with your printer. Press * (asterisk) to mark the font as `Present when print job begins` or press + (plus) to mark the font as `Can be loaded during print job.`

10. Press F7 (Exit) five times to return to the editing screen.

Fonts marked with both an asterisk (*) and plus sign (+)
are downloaded at the start of a print job and, if
necessary, unloaded in order to load another font. If you
unload the font, it will be loaded again at the end of the
job. To download soft fonts marked "initially present,"
press Shift-F7 (Print) and press 7 or I to choose
Initialize Printer.

Selecting fonts with + or * merely tells WordPerfect that
you intend to use that font. It does not mean that you
own the font. Fonts are optional and must be purchased.
Telling WordPerfect to use a font that is not installed
produces unpredictable results.

Printer Selection

Reminders

WordPerfect and the printer must be linked properly so
that the printer will print your documents.

A *printer definition* is not the same thing as a *printer*.
Printer definitions are software; printers are hardware.
A printer definition tells WordPerfect how to control a
certain make and model of printer. You may install and
have available for selection (from the Select Printer
menu) an unlimited number of printer definitions.

Printing

With WordPerfect, you can print directly from the screen
all or part of the document that currently appears, or you
can print all or part of a document you have previously
stored to disk. From the screen, you can print the entire
document, a single page, or a marked block of text.

To print the entire document from the screen

1. Place the cursor anywhere in the document.

2. Press Shift-F7 (Print) to display the Print menu.

3. Press 1 or F to choose the Full Document option.

To print a single page from the displayed document

1. Place the cursor where you want to print.

2. Press Shift-F7 (Print).

3. Press 2 or P to select Page.

If the page you selected does not appear near the beginning of the document, the printer may pause. WordPerfect scans the pages for the last format settings for margins, tabs, and so on.

To print a block of text from the screen

1. Move the cursor to the first character of the block of text you plan to print.

2. Press Alt-F4 or F12 (Block). The message `Block on` flashes in the lower left corner of your screen.

3. Move the cursor to the character space immediately following the last character of the block of text you plan to print.

4. Press Shift-F7 (Print). The prompt `Print block? No (Yes)` appears.

5. Press Y to print.

With WordPerfect, you can print a document from disk without displaying it on-screen. You can print from either the Print menu or the List Files menu.

Reminders

If the file you are printing is stored on a floppy disk, don't remove it from the disk drive until the print job has finished.

If you are using the Fast Save feature, you cannot print a document from the disk.

To use the Print menu to print a document from disk

1. Press **Shift-F7** (**Print**).

2. Press **3** or **D** to select Document on Disk. The prompt `Document name:` appears.

3. Type the file name and press **Enter**. Or, if the document is stored in a different directory than the current directory, type the drive, path, and file name, and press **Enter**.

4. Press **Enter** to print the entire document or type the pages you want to print and press **Enter**.

WordPerfect reads the file from disk, creates a print job, and adds the document to the print queue.

In addition to printing from the Print menu, you can print from the List Files screen. Printing from the List Files screen has two advantages: you don't need to remember the name of the file you want to print, and you can mark any number of files to print.

To use the List Files screen to print a document from disk

1. Press **F5** (**List Files**).

2. If the file resides in the current drive and directory, press **Enter**. Or, if the file is in a different directory, type the drive, path, and file name, and press **Enter**.

3. Use the cursor keys to highlight the name of the file you want to print.

4. Press **4** or **P** to select Print. `Pages: (All)` is displayed on the status line.

5. Press **Enter** to print the entire document or type the pages you want to print and press **Enter**.

To mark several files to print from the List Files screen

1. Press F5 (List Files).

2. Use the cursor keys to highlight the name of the file you want to print.

3. Press * (asterisk) to mark each file you want to print.

4. After you have marked each file, press 4 or P to select Print. WordPerfect prompts

   ```
   Print marked files? No (Yes)
   ```

5. Press Y.

WordPerfect adds the files to the printing queue and prints them in the order in which you selected the files.

WordPerfect's Control Printer feature is a powerful tool for managing your printing activities. You can cancel individual print jobs or all print jobs, display a list of jobs waiting to be printed, move a print job to the top of the list, and temporarily suspend and then resume printing if your printer has jammed.

To cancel a print job while it's printing

1. Press Shift-F7 (Print).

2. Press 4 or C to choose Control Printer and display the Control Printer menu.

3. Press 1 or C to choose Cancel Job(s). WordPerfect displays the following message (the number of the job currently printing is included in the prompt):

   ```
   Cancel which job? (*=All Jobs)
   ```

4. Press Enter to cancel the current job in the queue; or type the number of the job you want to cancel; or press * (asterisk) to cancel all the jobs in the queue and press Y to confirm the cancellation.

You can use the Rush Print Job option so that you can
print another job in the queue or print the rush job after
the current job is printed. If you elect to interrupt the job
currently printing, the document resumes printing after
the rush job is done.

To rush a print job

1. Press **Shift-F7** (**Print**).

2. Press **4** or **C** to select Control Printer.

3. Press **2** or **R** to select Rush Job. WordPerfect
   displays the following message:

   ```
   Rush which job?
   ```

4. Type the number of the print job you want to move
   up.

5. Press **Y** if you want to interrupt the current printing
   job, or press **N** or **Enter** to print the job after the
   current job is finished printing.

To stop printing temporarily

1. Press **Shift-F7** (**Print**).

2. Press **4** or **C** to select Control Printer.

3. Press **5** or **S** to choose Stop.

4. Make the desired corrections; then position the print
   head at the top of the next page.

5. Press **4** or **G** to choose Go (start printer). Printing
   resumes on page 1 if your document consists of
   only one page or if you stopped printing on page 1.
   Otherwise, WordPerfect prompts you to enter the
   page number where you want printing to resume.

6. Type the page number (if prompted) and press
   Enter

If you're printing on hand-fed single sheets or if you specified manual when you selected the printer, the printer does not start printing immediately after you have given the Print command. Instead, the printer pauses before printing each page to give you time to insert a sheet of paper. To start the first sheet, you must go back to the Control Printer screen.

To print on hand-fed paper

1. Press **Shift-F7** (**Print**).

2. Press **1** or **F** to select Full Document.

3. Press **Shift-F7** (**Print**) again.

4. Press **4** or **C** to choose Control Printer.

5. Press **4** or **G** to select Go once you have the paper aligned.

A sheet feeder supplies paper to the printer from one or more bins. Before you can use a sheet feeder, you must select a sheet feeder definition for your printer.

You select binding width, number of copies, and graphics and text quality from the Print menu.

WordPerfect will print the number of copies you selected for all print jobs until you change the Number of Copies option back to 1.

Binding width is the extra space added at the inside edge of each page when the document is printed. Setting a binding width shifts odd-numbered pages to the right and even-numbered pages to the left by the specified amount. The binding option provides an extra margin along the inside edge of the paper to allow for binding or three-hole drilling the final copy.

The Graphics Quality option controls the degree of resolution (sharpness) your printer uses to print graphics images.

The initial base font is the typeface style and sizes that WordPerfect uses to print standard text and around which other fonts are defined. Enhancements (boldface, italics, small caps, and so on) are variations of the current font. For example, if the current font is Times Roman and you use the Italics option on the Appearance menu, the text will be printed in Times Roman Italics.

To change the initial base font

1. Press Shift-F7 (Print).

2. Press S to choose Select Printer.

3. Use the cursor keys to highlight the name of the printer you want to edit.

4. Press 3 or E to choose Edit.

5. Press 5 or I to choose Initial Base Font. WordPerfect displays the Select Printer: Initial Font menu.

6. Use the cursor keys to highlight the name of a font and press Enter, 1, or S to select the font.

7. Press F7 (Exit) three times to return to the editing screen.

Redline and Strikeout

Redlining is a method of marking text you edited or added to a document. When several people work on a document, redlining is a useful way to let everyone know what changes are proposed.

In WordPerfect, you can choose how redlining appears on the printed page. With many printers, redline appears as a mark in the margin next to the redlined text. With other printers, redlined text appears shaded or highlighted. If you have a color printer, redlined text prints red.

Redlining is generally used for identifying text that needs to be expanded or illustrated. WordPerfect's *strikeout* feature, on the other hand, is used for identifying text that the editor believes should be deleted. Strikeout prints as dashes superimposed over other characters.

To select the redlining method

1. Press Shift-F8 (Format) to see the Format menu.

2. Press 3 or D to see the Format: Document menu.

3. Press 4 or R to select Redline Method.

4. Press 1 or P to select Printer Dependent, which marks redline text according to your printer's definition of redlining.

5. Press F7 (Exit) to return to your document.

To redline or strike out existing text

1. Press Alt-F4 or F12 (Block).

2. Highlight the block you want to redline or strike out.

3. Press Ctrl-F8 (Font). The Font menu appears at the bottom of your screen.

4. Press 2 or A to select Appearance.

5. Press 8 or R to select Redline or press 9 or S to select Strikeout.

Text marked for strikeout is not deleted until you generate your document by pressing Alt-F5 (Mark Text). To prevent text from being deleted, simply delete the [STKOUT] code.

Repeating Values

Some of the keys on your keyboard repeat when you
hold down the key. Many other WordPerfect functions
can be repeated only with the aid of the Esc key.

To repeat a character or a cursor-movement key

1. Move the cursor to the location where you want the
   character or cursor-movement key repeated.

2. Press Esc. The prompt Repeat Value=8
   appears in the lower left corner of the screen. The
   preset repeat value is 8, but it can be changed for
   one occurrence or for the entire work session.

3. Type the repeat value if 8 is not the correct number
   of repetitions.

4. Press the character or cursor-movement key to be
   repeated.

Retrieving Files

You can retrieve documents stored on disk in two ways:
press Shift-F10 (Retrieve) or press F5 (List) to use the
List Files screen. The List Files screen displays a two-
column alphabetized list of your files, including the file
size and the date and time each file was last saved.

Reminders

If you do not clear your screen before retrieving a
document, WordPerfect attaches the retrieved file to the
document displayed on-screen. Use F7 (Exit) to clear
the old document before retrieving the new document.

If you decide that you do not want to retrieve a file,
press F1 (Cancel).

To use the Retrieve command

1. Press **Shift-F10** (**Retrieve**). The following prompt is displayed:

   ```
   Document to be retrieved:
   ```

2. Type the name of the document and press **Enter**, or press **F5** (**List**). If the document is password-protected, WordPerfect prompts

   ```
   Enter Password (FILENAME):
   ```

3. Type the password and then press **Enter**.

If the message `ERROR: File Not Found` appears, either you typed the name incorrectly or the file doesn't exist in the directory. Type the name again. If you cannot remember the namet, use the List Files screen.

To use the List Files screen

1. Press **F5** (**List**). WordPerfect displays a file specification similar to the following in the lower left corner of the screen:

   ```
   Dir C:\WP50\*.*
   ```

2. To view the documents stored on the named drive, press **Enter**.

3. Use the arrow keys to move the highlight bar to the file you want to retrieve.

4. Press **1** or **R** to select the Retrieve option from the menu displayed at the bottom of your screen.

Reveal Codes

Many times when you press a key in WordPerfect, a *hidden code* is inserted into the text. The term *hidden* is used because you cannot see that code on-screen. Such codes tell WordPerfect when to execute tabs, margin settings, hard returns, indents, and so on. Some hidden codes turn on and off features, such as Math or Columns. And some codes work as a pair, such as the codes for bold, underline, and italic. The first code in a pair acts as a toggle switch to turn on a feature; the second code serves to turn off the feature. The feature used for displaying these codes is Reveal Codes.

To see the codes

1. Press Alt-F3 or F11 (Reveal Codes). The screen splits in half. The same text is displayed in both windows, but the text at the bottom half shows the hidden codes.

2. Press Alt-F3 or F11 (Reveal Codes) again to restore the normal screen.

You can change the size of the Reveal Codes portion of the screen permanently by pressing Alt-F1 (Setup), 2 or D (Display), 6 or E (Edit Screen Options), and 6 or R (Reveal Codes Window Size), and then entering a value. You can change this size for the current WordPerfect session only by pressing Ctrl-F3 (Screen), pressing 1 or W (Window), and then entering a value or using the ↑ or ↓ keys.

In Reveal Codes, the cursor in the lower window is a highlighted bar. When the cursor comes across a hidden code (in the lower window), the cursor expands to cover the entire code. In the upper window, you see only a blank space.

Hidden codes can be deleted in the normal typing screen or in the Reveal Codes screen. Because you can see the codes in the Reveal Codes screen, deleting them with Reveal Codes is easier.

As you delete codes from the Reveal Codes screen, notice that the effect of your changes is reflected in the upper portion of the screen. In Reveal Codes mode, you can enter commands and text and immediately observe the position of any new hidden codes.

To delete codes

1. Move the cursor to the place in your document where the code is likely to be located.

2. Press Alt-F3 or F11 (Reveal Codes).

3. Position the cursor on the hidden code.

4. Press Del to delete the hidden code.

5. To return to the normal typing screen, press Alt-F3 or F11 (Reveal Codes) again.

Saving Documents

What you see on-screen is a *temporary* display; only the documents you transferred to disk storage enjoy a measure of security. If something interrupts the power to your computer (a storm, a power cord pulled from the wall, or a power surge, for example), any unsaved text is gone forever.

Use the Setup feature to configure WordPerfect to save your work every 10 or 15 minutes. Press Shift-F1 (Setup), 3 or E (Environment), 1 or B (Backup Options), and 1 or T (Timed Document Backup). Answer yes and enter a time interval. Document 1 is saved as WP{WP}.BK1, and document 2 is saved as WP{WP}.BK2. These backups are temporary and are erased when you exit from WordPerfect. Their sole purpose is to protect you in case of system or power failure. To use a backup, rename it and then retrieve it.

File names have two parts. The first part of the name can contain from one to eight characters (numbers, letters, and some punctuation marks). The second part (called the *extension*) can contain no more than three characters. The first part of the file name is separated from its extension by a period (.). For example, in the file name LETTER1.JIM, the extension is .JIM. Use the extension to categorize files.

If you are using a hard disk system, the program, system, and document files usually reside on drive C. When you press F10 (Save) or F7 (Exit), the prompt includes the disk drive and directory designation.

Most hard disk drive users make subdirectories to organize and store different kinds of documents. For example, you may have a subdirectory called WPLETTER in which you save correspondence or a subdirectory called WPMEMO in which you save interoffice memos. WordPerfect permits you to create directories with the List Files feature.

On a two-floppy disk system, drive A is reserved for program and system data. Do not save documents on drive A. Instead, start the program from drive A and make drive B your default drive for your documents.

To save and name your documents

1. Press F10 (Save) or F7 (Exit). The following prompt appears:

   ```
   Document to be saved:
   ```

2. Press Enter to keep the name that appears in the prompt. Or, to save the file in the current directory, type a file name and press Enter. To save the file in another subdirectory, type the path name and the file name and press Enter.

   ```
   Replace C:\WP\LETTER.JLS No (Yes)
   ```

3. If you want to replace the old file with the file on-screen, press Y.

If you press F10, you are automatically returned to the document. If you press F7, you can leave WordPerfect by pressing Y, clear the screen by pressing N, or return by pressing F1 (Cancel).

The Screen Display

The line of information that appears at the bottom of the editing screen is called the *status line*. The left side of the status line shows the current document's name. From time to time, the document name is replaced temporarily by system messages and prompts.

The second item on the status line (Doc) indicates which of two available documents is currently displayed on-screen. WordPerfect is able to hold two documents in memory simultaneously. The documents are identified as either Doc 1 or Doc 2.

Pg identifies the number of the page on which the cursor currently rests.

Ln indicates the vertical distance from the top edge of the page, in inches, centimeters, points, or lines (on your document page), on which the cursor rests. You can change the units used by selecting that option on the Setup menu (press Shift-F1 to display the Setup menu).

Pos tells you the horizontal distance in from the left edge of the page. The Pos indicator serves the following functions as well: (1) the Pos indicator appears in uppercase letters (POS) if the Caps Lock key is activated for typing in uppercase letters; (2) when the Pos indicator blinks, the Num Lock key is activated so that you can use the numeric keypad to type numbers; (3) when you create or move through boldface letters, the position indicator number changes from regular type to boldface type; (4) when the cursor moves into

underlined or double-underlined text, the position
indicator number reflects the enhancement of the text.

Status line information appears only on-screen; it does
not appear in your printed document.

WordPerfect's screen displays only text and does not
show your document exactly as it will be printed. To
preview a page, press Shift-F7 (Print) and then press 6
or V (View Document). Your computer must be capable
of displaying graphics.

Search and Replace

The Search feature enables you to search for a single
character, word, phrase, sentence, or hidden codes in
either a forward or reverse direction from the location of
your cursor. The group of characters or words you want
to locate is called a *search string*.

WordPerfect differentiates between upper- and
lowercase characters only if you type uppercase
characters in the search string. If you type the string in
lowercase, WordPerfect looks for either upper- or
lowercase characters. For example, if you ask the
program to find *search*, WordPerfect stops at *search*,
Search, and *SEARCH*. But if you ask the program to find
SEARCH, WordPerfect stops only at the word *SEARCH*.

Reminders

Be careful how you enter a search string. For example, if
you enter the string the, WordPerfect matches your
string to every occurrence of the word *the* as well as
words that contain the string, such as anes*the*sia. To
locate only the word *the*, enter a space before and after
the word: <space>the<space>.

If you think that the string you're looking for may be in a header, footer, footnote, endnote, graphic box caption, or text box, you must perform an *extended search*. An extended search is the same as a regular search except that you must press Home and then F2 for an extended forward search and Home and then Shift-F2 for an extended backward search.

If you need to find a hidden code, such as a margin setting, use the normal search procedure, but when the Srch: prompt appears, press the function key that creates the hidden code. When the search finds the hidden code, press Alt-F3 (Reveal Codes) to view the code and perform any editing.

When searching for paired codes, you can insert an ending code at the search (or replace) prompt by pressing the corresponding function key twice; for example, press F6 (Bold) once to insert a [BOLD] code and twice to insert [bold]. To remove the [BOLD] code, delete it with the cursor and Del keys.

If you are searching for text that includes an element that changes from one occurrence to the next—for example, (1), (2), (3)—or if you are uncertain about the correct spelling of a word, use the matching character ^X (press Ctrl-V, Ctrl-X). This *wildcard* character matches any single character within a character string. Enter (^X) at the Srch: prompt, and the cursor will stop at (1), (2), (3), (4), and so on. When you are uncertain about the spelling, enter c^Xt at the Srch: prompt, and the cursor will stop at *cat, CAT, Cat, cot, cattle, cutting,* and so on. Be as specific about your character string as you can.

To find a word at the end of a paragraph, type the word at the Srch: prompt, along with any following punctuation, and then press Enter to insert a [HRt] code. For example, type Einstein.[HRt]. The search finds only occurrences of Einstein that are followed by a period and a hard return (Enter key).

To use Search

1. Press F2 (Forward Search) to search from the cursor position forward to the end of the document or press Shift-F2 (Backward Search) to search from the end of the document to the beginning.

2. Type the text string or code you want to find. You may type as many as 60 characters.

3. Press F2 or Esc to begin the search.

When WordPerfect finds the first occurrence of the search target, the search stops. You can edit and move around in the document freely.

If you want to continue the search, repeat Steps 1 and 3. You don't need to retype your search string or code because WordPerfect remembers your last search request.

If WordPerfect cannot find the search text, a
`* Not Found *` message is displayed.

To return the cursor to its location before the search, press Ctrl-Home (GoTo) twice.

Caution

A common mistake is to press Enter rather than F2 (Forward Search) or Esc to exit the `Srch:` prompt. Pressing Enter inserts a `[HRt]` code in the search string, which may not be what you intended.

WordPerfect's Replace feature finds every occurrence of a string or hidden code and replaces it with another string or code. You also can use Replace to remove a string or code completely.

To replace a string

1. Press Alt-F2 (Replace). The following prompt appears in the lower left corner of the screen:

`w/Confirm? No (Yes)`

2. Press **Y** if you want to approve each replacement separately or press **N** or **Enter** if you do not want to confirm all occurrences.

3. At the → `Srch:` prompt, type your search string.

4. Press **F2** (**Forward Search**) or **Esc.** The following prompt appears:

    `Replace with:`

5. If you want the string replaced, type the replacement string. If not, go directly to Step 6.

6. Press **F2** (**Forward Search**) or **Esc.**

7. To return to the position of the cursor before the Replace operation began, press **Ctrl-Home** twice.

To replace hidden codes

1. Press **Alt-F2** (**Replace**).

2. Press **Y** if you want to confirm each replacement or press **N** if you want all occurrences replaced.

3. When the → `Srch:` prompt appears, press the function key you would use to initiate the desired command—for example, press **F6** (**Bold**).

4. At the `Replace with:` prompt, type the replacement string. Or, to delete the hidden code and replace it with nothing, go directly to Step 5.

5. Press **F2** (**Forward Search**) to begin the Replace operation.

Sort and Select

WordPerfect's Sort and Select feature has enough power and versatility to handle most record-keeping tasks. Examples of two simple applications of the Sort command are sorting lines to create alphabetical phone lists or rosters, and sorting mailing lists by ZIP code to conform with postal service rules for large mailings.

WordPerfect can maneuver three kinds of records: a line, a paragraph, or a secondary merge file. A line record ends with a hard or soft return, and a paragraph record ends with two hard returns. A secondary merge file contains records, each of which has fields. A field ends with an {END FIELD} merge code, and a record ends with an {END RECORD} merge code.

Before you tell WordPerfect how you want to sort or select information, you need to understand the terms used by these functions.

You can sort files displayed on-screen or files stored on disk, and you can return the sorted results to the screen or to a new file on disk. Sort works with three kinds of data: a line, paragraph, and secondary merge file. Use line sort when records are lines (a name or an item, for example), use paragraph sort when records are paragraphs (as in a standard legal clause, perhaps), and use merge sort when records are a secondary merge file (a list of names and addresses, for example).

To perform a sort

1. If you want to sort a file while it's displayed, retrieve the desired file to your screen.

2. Press Ctrl-F9 (Merge/Sort). WordPerfect displays the Merge/Sort menu.

3. Press 2 or S to choose Sort. The following prompt appears in the lower left corner of the screen:

   ```
   Input file to sort: (Screen)
   ```

4. Press Enter if you want to sort the file displayed. Or type the input file name if you want to sort a file stored on disk.and then press Enter The following prompt appears in the lower left corner of the screen:

   ```
   Output file for sort: (Screen)
   ```

5. Press Enter if you want the sorted results to replace the screen display or type the output file name if you want the sorted results saved to a new file.

6. Press 7 or T to choose Type. WordPerfect displays the Type menu:

```
Type: 1 Merge; 2 Line; 3
Paragraph: 0
```

7. Select the type of records you are sorting: a secondary merge file (1), document lines (2), or paragraphs (3).

8. Press 6 or O to choose Order. WordPerfect displays the Direction menu.

9. Press 1 or A to choose Ascending for A-to-Z sort order or press 2 or D to choose Descending for Z-to-A sort order.

10. Press 3 or K to choose Keys. WordPerfect displays the Keys menu:

```
Type: a = Alphanumeric; n =
Numeric; Use arrows; Press Exit
when done
```

11. Press A to specify an alphanumeric sort for Key1 or press N to specify a numeric sort for Key1.

12. Enter the location of Key1.

13. To sort a list of names where the first and last names, such as *John Smith*, are together in a single field (no tab in between), enter **-1** for the word to tell WordPerfect to sort on the first word counting from right to left.

14. If you want to sort on more than one field, press the → key to move to the entry area for Key2.

15. Enter the key location for Key2.

16. Move to and enter information for other keys.

17. Press **F7** (Exit) to go to the Sort and Select menu.

18. To start the sort, press **1** or **P**.

WordPerfect can sort the lines and paragraphs in any standard text file. This feature is particularly useful when you want to sort through office phone lists, personnel rosters, columns on charts, dated paragraphs, glossaries, and so on. Sort lines when you plan to sort rosters and lists. Use paragraph sort when sorting notes or reports.

To sort lines

1. Retrieve a file to the screen.

2. Press **Ctrl-F9** (Merge/Sort).

3. Press **2** or **S** to choose Sort.

4. Press **Enter** to sort the file displayed on-screen. Or type the input file name to sort a file stored on disk.

5. Press **Enter** if you want the sorted results to replace the screen display or type the output file name to save the results to disk in a new file.

6. Press **7** or **T** to choose Type.

7. Press **2** or **L** to choose Line. The title on the Sort screen is now Sort by Line, and the key location headings are Field and Word. Identify the location of key words by their Field and Word numbers in each line. Fields are separated by tabs, and words are separated by spaces.

8. After entering the key locations, press **F7** (Exit) to return to the main Sort and Select menu.

9. Press **1** or **P** to choose Perform Action. WordPerfect sorts the file and sends the results to the screen or to the file, as specified in Step 5.

To sort paragraphs

1. Retrieve your file to the screen to perform the sort while the document is displayed.

2. Press Ctrl-F9 (Merge/Sort).

3. Press 2 or S to choose Sort.

4. Press Enter to sort the file displayed on-screen. Or type the input file name to sort a file stored on disk.

5. Press Enter if you want the sorted results to replace the screen display or type the output file name if you want the sorted results saved to a new file.

6. At the Sort and Select menu, press 7 or T to choose Type.

7. Press 3 or P to choose Paragraph. The heading on the main Sort screen changes to Sort by Paragraph, and the key location headings change to Line, Field, and Word. Paragraphs are separated by two or more hard returns.

8. Press F7 (Exit) to return to the Sort and Select menu.

9. Press 1 or P for Perform Action.

A secondary merge file is nothing more than a database with implanted merge codes. WordPerfect can sort your secondary merge files so that the form letters, mailing lists, or labels you previously typed print in any order.

To sort merge files

1. Retrieve your file to the screen.

2. Press Ctrl-F9 (Merge/Sort).

3. Press 2 or S to choose Sort.

4. Press Enter if you want to sort the file displayed on-screen. Or type the input file name if you want to sort a file stored on disk.

5. Press Enter if you want the sorted results to replace the screen display or type the output file name if you want the sorted results saved to a new file.

6. At the Sort and Select menu, press 7 or T to choose Type.

7. Press 1 or M to choose Merge. The location headings for each key become Field, Line, and Word, and the screen heading becomes Sort Secondary Merge File.

8. Press 3 or K to choose Keys.

9. Press the right or left arrow to move between keys.

10. Press F7 (Exit) to return to the Sort and Select menu.

11. Press 1 or P to select Perform Action. WordPerfect sorts the file based on your sort criteria.

When you work with a large database, you often need to select only particular data, and you must be precise about your selection. Using the Select feature (included in WordPerfect's Sort menu), you can choose only those paragraphs, lines, or secondary merge records that contain a specific combination of data—for example, the names of customers who live in Texas. The steps for selecting are the same as those for sorting, but you must include a statement that describes the records you want to select.

A simple selection statement may be

```
Key1=perkins
```

This selection statement tells WordPerfect to select only those records in which the last name is *perkins* or *Perkins*. (WordPerfect's Sort and Select features do not distinguish between upper- and lowercase.)

Special Characters

You can use WordPerfect's Compose features to enter special characters. A full listing of characters and symbols supported by WordPerfect appears in the WordPerfect manual.

To create special characters with Compose

1. Press Ctrl-V. The following prompt appears:

   ```
   Key =
   ```

2. Type the the number of the character set, a comma, and then the number of the character; then press Enter

Or, if the character is a combination of two characters, type the first character and then type the second character. For example, type a c and a comma (,) to yield a French cedilla (ç).

You can manufacture your own special characters with WordPerfect's Overstrike feature. For example, you can create a zero with a slash through it by printing a 0 and / at the same location.

To create special characters with Overstrike

1. Move the cursor to the point where you want to create an overstrike character.

2. Press Shift-F8 (Format) .

3. Press 4 or O to select Other.

4. Press 5 or O to select Overstrike.

5. Press 1 or C to choose Create.

6. Type each character (or attribute) you want to appear in that character position.

7. Press Enter. You can see the characters and codes, but when you return to your document, only the last character you entered is visible.

8. Press F7 (Exit) to return to your document.

The characters you entered will be printed in the same character position. To review the codes and characters, press Alt-F3 or F11 for Reveal Codes.

Superscript and subscript are font attributes located on the Font: Size menu. A *superscript* is a number or letter written immediately above, or above and to the right or left of, another character. A *subscript* is a distinguishing symbol written immediately below, or below and to the right or left of, another character.

To create a subscript or superscript character

1. Press Ctrl-F8 (Font).

2. Press 1 or S to select Size.

3. Press 1 or P to select Superscript or press 2 or B to select Subscript.

4. Type the super- or subscripted characters.

5. Press the right-arrow key to move the cursor one character to the right when you want to return to the normal font.

If the text to be super- or subscripted is already typed, press Alt-F4 or F12 to define it as a block, press Ctrl-F8 (the Font key), press 1 or S to select Size, and then choose the appropriate appearance.

Spell Checking

WordPerfect's Speller contains a dictionary with more than 115,000 words. Use the Speller to search for spelling mistakes and common typing errors such as transposed, missing, extra, or wrong letters—even typing errors such as double words (*the the*). You also can use the Speller when you know what a word sounds like but you're unsure of its spelling. WordPerfect's Speller checks a single word, a page, a block of text, or an entire document. The Speller also checks for unusual capitalization (*tHe*, for example).

The Speller compares each word in your document with the words in its dictionary. This dictionary contains a list of *common* words (words most frequently used) and a list of *main* words (words generally found in dictionaries). WordPerfect checks every word against its list of common words, and if the program doesn't find the word there, it looks in its dictionary of main words. If you add your own words, the program looks in this supplemental dictionary as well.

Reminder

If your WordPerfect program is loaded on the hard disk, the Spell files are immediately available. For the Spell function to work correctly, the files must be in the dictionary specified in the Setup, Location of Files screen.

To start the Speller on a dual-floppy disk system

1. Be sure that you saved in drive B the document you want to check.

2. Remove the data disk from drive B and insert your copy of the Speller disk. (Do not remove the WordPerfect Program disk from drive A.)

3. When you finish checking spelling, put your working disk back into drive B.

To check a word, page, or entire document

1. If you plan to check just a word or a page, place the cursor anywhere in the word or page. If you plan to check the entire document, the position of the cursor does not matter.

2. If you are using a floppy disk system, remove the data disk from drive B and insert the Speller disk.

3. Press Ctrl-F2 (Spell). The Spell menu appears at the bottom of the screen:

```
Check: 1 Word; 2 Page; 3
Document; 4 New Sup. Dictionary;
5 Look Up; 6 Count: 0
```

4. Press the number or letter of your menu selection.

If you press 1 or W for Word, WordPerfect checks its dictionaries for that word. If WordPerfect finds the word, the cursor moves to the next word in your document, and the Spell menu remains displayed. You can continue checking word by word or select another option from the Spell menu. If the word isn't found, WordPerfect offers alternate spellings.

If you press 2 or P for Page, WordPerfect looks up every word on the page. After the page is checked, the Spell menu remains displayed. Continue checking words or select another option.

If you press 3 or D for Document, WordPerfect looks up every word in your document.

If you press 4 or N for New Sup. Dictionary, you can use a supplemental dictionary by typing the name of the dictionary and pressing Enter. Generally, these dictionaries contain words pertaining to specialized or technical areas, such as medicine, law, or science.

If you press 5 or L for Look Up, WordPerfect checks a word you aren't sure how to spell. In response to the prompt, type your "rough guess" of the word's spelling. WordPerfect offers a list of words that fit the pattern.

If you press 6 or C for Count, WordPerfect counts the number of words checked in a given check. To know how many words are contained in your document, spell-check the entire document or select Count.

To spell-check a block of text, use WordPerfect's Block feature to highlight the block and then press Ctrl-F2 (Spell).

When the Speller cannot find a word, the Speller stops, highlights the word, and usually provides a list of alternative spellings.

To select a word from the alternatives list

1. Find the correct spelling among the list of alternatives. If you do not see the correct spelling and WordPerfect prompts Press Enter for More Words, do so.

2. Type the letter next to the alternative spelling you want to select.

After you correct the word, the Speller continues checking the rest of your document. WordPerfect gives you several other options. For a discussion of these options, see the next section.

Many correctly spelled words do not appear in WordPerfect's dictionary. When the Speller notes a word as incorrect, the Not Found menu is displayed:

```
Not Found: 1 Skip Once; 2 Skip;
3 Add Word; 4 Edit; 5 Look Up: 0
```

If you select Skip (2), the Speller ignores what you know to be a correctly spelled word for the remainder of the document and continues the check. If you select Skip Once (1), the Speller ignores the word once but stops at every subsequent occurrence of the word. Skip Once allows you to verify your spelling of the word.

If a word you use frequently is not in WordPerfect's dictionary, select Add Word (3); WordPerfect stores the word in memory and approves all future occurrences as the spell check continues. At the end of the check, all

words added are saved to the current supplemental
dictionary file on disk.

When the correct alternative is not offered and when you
know the spelling is incorrect, you must correct the word
yourself. You can select Edit (4) and then make the
necessary corrections. Or you can select Look Up (5) to
display additional alternatives.

In addition to identifying misspelled words, the Speller
notes double words, such as *the the*. When the Speller
encounters a double word, the program doesn't offer
alternatives. Instead, the following menu is displayed:

```
Double Word: 1 2 Skip; 3 Delete
2nd; 4 Edit; 5 Disable Double
Word Checking
```

If you accidentally type two words rather than one,
select Delete 2nd (3). Select Skip (1 or 2) if the double
word is legitimate. If one of the words contains a typing
error, select Edit (4) and make the appropriate
corrections. If your document contains many legitimate
double words and you are certain of your proofreading
skill, select Disable Double Word Checking (5). The
Speller continues to check the rest of your text.

To edit a word manually

1. Press 4 or E for Edit, and the cursor moves to the
   word.

2. Make the corrections using the right- and left-arrow
   keys. You can move only in the line containing the
   word to be corrected.

3. Press F7 (Exit). The Speller rechecks the word you
   corrected. If the corrected version is not in the
   dictionary, the Speller stops.

To look up a word

1. Press 5 or L for Look Up.

2. Type the word or word pattern and press Enter.

3. Press F7 (Exit) twice to return to your document or enter another word or word pattern.

To check a block

1. Press Alt-F4 or F12 (Block) and define the block you want to check.

2. Press Ctrl-F2 (Spell).

When you spell-check a block, you skip the Spell menu because you already told WordPerfect how much of your document you plan to check. Otherwise, the Speller operates as usual.

WordPerfect checks the first three letters of each word for unusual capitalization. *ThE* and *dBASE* are considered unusual, but *IBM* is not.

Press 1 or 2 to accept the word as is, 3 to replace according to WordPerfect's own capitalization rules, 4 to edit the word, or 5 to turn off the process.

Spreadsheet Importing

Spreadsheet files from Lotus 1-2-3, Excel, and PlanPerfect can be used directly in WordPerfect documents without the need for conversion.

You can *import* a spreadsheet, a one-time operation that enters the spreadsheet data into your document as regular text, or you can create a *link*, which actually reads the spreadsheet file every time you retrieve your WordPerfect document so your document is always up to date.

To import a spreadsheet

1. Press Ctrl-F5 (Text In/Out).

2. Press 5 or S for Spreadsheet.

3. Press 1 or I for Import.

4. Press **1** or **F** for Filename.

5. Type the spreadsheet file name or press **F5** (**List**) to highlight and retrieve a file.

6. Specify the cell range or named range you want to import. Leaving this option blank causes the entire spreadsheet to be imported.

7. Select whether you want to import the spreadsheet into a WordPerfect table (preferred) or as text formatted with tabs. If you choose to import the spreadsheet into a table, it is created automatically.

8. Press **4** or **P** to perform the import.

To link a spreadsheet

1. Press **Ctrl-F5** (**Text In/Out**).

2. Press **5** or **S** for Spreadsheet.

3. Press **2** or **C** for Create Link.

4. Press **1** or **F** for Filename.

5. Type the spreadsheet file name or press **F5** (**List**) to highlight and retrieve a file.

6. Specify the cell range or named range you want to import. Leaving this option blank causes the entire spreadsheet to be imported.

7. Select whether you want to import the spreadsheet into a WordPerfect table (preferred) or as text formatted with tabs. If you choose to import the spreadsheet into a table, it is created automatically.

8. Press **4** or **P** to perform the link.

You also can edit an existing link and modify link options.

Starting WordPerfect

If you are using a hard disk system

1. At the DOS C> prompt, type CD\WP51 and press Enter.

2. Type WP and press Enter to start WordPerfect.

If you are using a dual-floppy disk system

1. Insert into drive A either your 5 1/4-inch WordPerfect 1 (sys)—Working disk or your 3 1/2-inch WordPerfect 1/WordPerfect 2 (sys)—Working disk.

2. Insert a blank, formatted disk into drive B. This disk will store your documents.

3. At the DOS A> prompt, type B: and press Enter to change to drive B.

4. Type A:WP and press Enter.

5. If you have 5 1/4-inch disks, replace the disk labeled WordPerfect 1 (sys)—Working with the disk labeled WordPerfect 2 (sys)—Working.

Styles

You can use Style (Alt-F8) as a powerful tool to control the format of one document or a group of documents. A *style* is a group of WordPerfect codes (you can include text also) that you turn on and off to control the format of your document. For example, a style may contain all the codes needed for you to format a chapter heading or a long quotation. You can save style definitions with the current document, or you can save them to a style library file to use on other documents. Styles improve your productivity because every time you change the codes in the style, the program updates every occurrence of that style in your document.

WordPerfect's styles fall into three categories: *open*, *paired*, and *outline*. Open styles remain in effect until you override the style codes, either by using another style or by inserting other formatting codes manually. Use open styles for formatting that affects an entire document. If the style is to affect the entire document, move the cursor to the beginning of the document before turning on the style.

Paired styles are turned on and off. You can create a paired style called Heading that makes the text bold and italic. When you use this style, you insert [Style On: Heading] and [Style Off: Heading] codes around the text to be formatted. Use paired styles for any text element that has a beginning and an end.

An outline style is actually a set of eight separate styles that correspond to the eight possible levels in an outline.

To create a style

1. Press Alt-F8 (Style) to display the Styles menu.

2. Press 3 or C for Create.

3. Enter a name for the style, select a type (open, paired, or outline), and enter a description.

4. Press 4 or C for Codes and enter the hidden codes and text you want included in the style. Press F7 (Exit) when you're finished.

Redefine the Enter key to turn a paired style off or on. The latter is especially useful for a style that creates a numbered, indented paragraph.

To use a style

1. Move the cursor to where you want the style to begin.

2. Press Alt-F8 (Style) to display the Styles menu.

3. Use the cursor keys to highlight the style you want to use.

4. Press 1 or O or Enter to turn on the style.

5. Type your text.

If you are using a paired style and defined Enter as Off, the style is turned off when you press Enter. If you are using a paired style and defined Enter as HRt or On/Off, the style is turned off when you press Alt-F8 (Style) and press 2 or F.

To use a paired style with existing text, press Alt-F4 or F12 (Block), highlight the text, and then follow Steps 1–4 for using a style.

When you save your document, the style definitions are saved with your document regardless of whether you used them. Whenever you edit this document, the styles are available for use. You also can save style definitions to a style library; then you can use these styles on other documents.

You can use the style library (LIBRARY.STY) found on WordPerfect's Conversion disk, or you can create a style library yourself. Also, you can set up one style library as your default.

Tables

The Tables feature allows you to create a spreadsheet type of grid with or without lines. You can perform four-function math or enter text into the individual cells. Each cell supports word wrap adjusting its height to the number of text rows and font. You can join several cells into one larger cell or split cells into additional rows or columns. You also can import spreadsheet files into a table (see "Spreadsheet Importing").

You may find that working with tables is easier than using math or parallel columns.

To create a table

1. Press Alt-F7 (Columns/Tables).

2. Press 2 or T for Tables.

3. Press 1 or C for Create.

4. Type the number of columns you want and press Enter.

5. Type the number of rows you want and press Enter.

WordPerfect draws a grid on the screen with the appropriate number of rows and columns.

You remain in the table editor, which allows you to format the table. To enter text into the table, you must first press F7 (Exit) to leave the table editor and return to the regular editing screen.

Rows, columns, individual cells, or blocks can be formatted .

In order to perform the functions that follow, you must make sure that the table editor is active. Activate the table editor by moving the cursor to any cell in the table and then pressing Alt-F7 (Columns/Tables).

To add more rows and columns

1. Position the cursor.

2. Press Alt-F7 (Columns/Tables).

3. Press the Ins key.

4. Press 1 or R to insert rows. Press 2 or C to insert columns.

5. Type the number of rows or columns to add and press Enter.

Deleting rows or columns is a similar process; just press
Del rather than Ins .

You can combine several cells to make a large cell for a
title or divide cells to create additional cells.

To join cells

1. Press Alt-F7 (Columns/Tables).

2. Position the cursor where you want to begin.

3. Press Alt-F4 (Block) and highlight the cells to be
   joined.

4. Press 7 or J for Join.

5. Press Y in response to the `Join Cells? No
   (Yes)` prompt.

To split cells

1. Press Alt-F7 (Columns/Tables).

2. Position the cursor where you want to begin.

3. Press Alt-F4 (Block) and highlight the cells to be
   split.

4. Press 8 or P for Split.

5. Press 1 or C to create columns or press 2 or R to
   create rows.

6. Enter the number of columns or rows you want to
   create and press Enter.

You can designate rows from your table to print as a
header at the top of each page when your table extends
over several pages.

To create a table header

1. Press Alt-F7 (Columns/Tables).

2. Position the cursor at the cell you want to use as a
   header.

3. Press 4 or H for Header.

4. Type the number of rows to be used as a header and press Enter.

The status line displays an asterisk next to the cell name to indicate that it is part of a header.

To duplicate the functions provided by WordPerfect's Parallel Columns feature, you may want to make the lines of the table invisible.

To make all the lines invisible

1. Press Alt-F7.

2. Move the cursor to a corner cell.

3. Press Alt-F4 (Block) or F12 and use the End and arrow keys to highlight the entire table.

4. Press 3 or L for Lines.

5. Press 7 or A for All.

6. Press 1 or N for None.

Tab Stops

Two classes of tabs exist in WordPerfect: *absolute* and *relative*. Absolute tabs are always measured from the left edge of the paper and do not adjust if you change the left margin. All versions of WordPerfect prior to 5.1 offer only absolute tabs. Relative tabs are tied to the left margin setting and float as you change the margin. Relative tabs are the default in Version 5.1.

WordPerfect comes with tab stops predefined at one-half inch intervals. Four basic kinds of tabs are available: left, center, right, and decimal. In addition, each type of tab can have a *dot leader* (a series of dots before the tab). The following table explains the types of tabs available.

Tab Type	*Operation*
Left (L)	Indent to tab stop; text continues right. Left tab is the most commonly used tab stop.
Center (C)	Text is centered at tab stop. Center tab works much the same as Shift-F6 (Center), but can force centering anywhere on the line. Use center tabs to create column headings.
Right (R)	After a right tab stop, text continues to the left. Right tab stop is similar to Alt-F6 (Flush Right), but right tab stops can be placed anywhere on the line. Use right tab to create headings over columns of numbers and dates.
Decimal (D)	After a decimal tab stop, text continues to the left until the alignment character is typed; then text continues to the right. Decimal tab stops are similar to Ctrl-F6 (Tab Align), but you preset the alignment character as a tab stop. The default alignment character is a period (.), but you can change it to any character). Use decimal tabs to line up columns of numbers.
Dot Leaders (.)	Any of the four tab types can be preceded by dots (periods) as leaders. Use dot leaders for long lists that require scanning from left to right (phone lists, for example).

You can change tab settings for all documents or for only the document on which you're currently working.

You can set tab stops one at a time, or specify the increment and set several tab stops at once. Similarly, you can delete one tab stop, all tab stops, or only the tab stops to the right of the cursor. You can set multiple tab stops across 8.5 inches of your page. If you print on wider paper, you can extend tab stops from 8.5 inches to 54.5 inches, but you must set those stops individually. You can set a maximum of 40 tab stops.

To view current tab stop settings, use the Window feature to display the tab ruler.

To display the tab ruler

1. Press Ctrl-F3 (Screen).

2. Press 1 or W for Window.

3. Type a number that is one less than the one displayed in the prompt.

4. Press Enter.

A tab ruler appears at the bottom of your screen. The curly braces mark the left and right margins. (Instead of braces, you may see brackets. The brackets indicate that a tab stop and margin setting occur at the same location.) The triangles mark the tab stops.

To erase the tab ruler, repeat Steps 1 and 2. For Step 3, type a number one greater than the value displayed.

To change the tab stops

1. Press Shift-F8 (Format).

2. Press 1 or L to display the Format: Line menu.

3. Press 8 or T to select Tab Set and to see the tab ruler.

4. To delete a single tab stop, use the cursor keys to move to the tab you want to delete and press Del or Backspace .

5. Press T for Type and choose absolute or relative tabs. Relative tabs are shown on the tab ruler with + and – signs to indicate the distance on either side of the left margin.

6. To add a single tab stop, use the cursor keys to move to the position where you want a tab stop and press the appropriate tab type: L to add a left tab, C to add a center tab, R to add a right tab, or D to add a decimal tab. To add a dot leader, press . (period).

7. Press F7 (Exit) twice to return to your document.

You can center text on a regular tab stop by pressing Home and then Shift- F6 (Center) to move the cursor to that tab location.

Tables of Authorities

The term *table of authorities* may be unfamiliar unless you work with legal briefs or scholarly manuscripts. A table of authorities is a list of court cases, rules of court, statutes, agency opinions, and miscellaneous authorities mentioned in a document. Each type of authority is usually assigned its own section in the table. Within each section, the citations are listed alphabetically.

Your table of authorities can contain up to 16 sections. Enter the first reference (or *full form*) of the authority in a special editing screen. Then, if you have subsequent references to the same citation, give them a unique *short form* identifier so that WordPerfect can collect these subsequent references and compile them in a table with their page references. You can mark authorities in footnotes, endnotes, and graphics boxes, as well as in the body text.

After you mark the authorities, use the Mark Text key to enter a definition code that tells WordPerfect where and in what format to generate the table of authorities.

Each section of a table of authorities is alphabetized separately; therefore, you can set up separate lists of case citations, constitutional citations, and legal citations. You must define each section separately.

Tables of Contents

When you create a table of contents, WordPerfect generally uses text taken directly from the document—chapter headings, for example. Creating a table of contents is similar to generating an index: you mark the text to be included in the table of contents, define the style, and then generate the table of contents.

WordPerfect inserts a [Mark:ToC,1] code at the beginning of the marked text and an [End Mark: ToC,n] code at the end. To omit the marked item from the table of contents, delete one code; WordPerfect deletes the other code for you. Formatting codes (underline and boldface codes, for example) are included in the table of contents if you include them when you mark the text.

You can change any or all of the following options:

Number of Levels: Select this option, type the number of levels you want to include in your table of contents, and press **Enter**.

Display Last Level in Wrapped Format: Choose this option and press **Y** if you want to display the last level of the table of contents in wrapped format. Press **N** if you don't want this option turned on.

Select Page Number Position: Use this option to specify one of the following page number positions for each of your levels: None, Pg # Follows, (Pg #) Follows, Flush Rt, or Flush Rt with Leader. (You may not choose a flush-right style for the last level if you have specified that the line will word wrap.)

When you define the table of contents, WordPerfect enters a code that reflects the options you selected—for example, [Def Mark:ToC,3:4,5,5]. The table of contents will be generated at this mark.

To generate a table of contents, press **Alt-F5 (Mark Text)** and follow the prompts.

By creating a style for each level in a table of contents, you can format the headings in your document and modify the formats, if necessary.

The Thesaurus

The Thesaurus contains *synonyms*—words with the same or similar meanings—and *antonyms*—words with opposite or nearly opposite meanings. The Thesaurus only lists these words; you must decide which one most closely fits your meaning. If you are not certain of the correct spelling, use the asterisk (*) and the question mark (?) to check the word and then use the Thesaurus.

The word you look up is called the *headword* because it has a body of similar words attached to it. The headword appears at the top of the column. Synonyms and antonyms marked with a bullet also are headwords; you can look up any of these words for more ideas.

To use the Thesaurus

1. If you are using a floppy disk system, remove the data disk from drive B and insert the Thesaurus disk. The WordPerfect Program disk must remain in drive A.

2. Place the cursor anywhere in the word you want to look up and press Alt-F1 (Thesaurus).

3. To replace the highlighted word, press 1 for Replace Word.

4. Type the letter that corresponds to the replacement word. The Thesaurus menu disappears, and the program inserts the word you selected into the text.

5. If you are using a floppy disk system, remove the Thesaurus disk, replace it with your data disk, and save your document.

To display synonyms for a word preceded by a bullet, simply type the highlighted letter that appears next to the bullet. To select words from the second and third columns, press → to move the highlighted letters.

To view other words

1. Press Alt-F1 (Thesaurus).

2. Press 3 for Look Up Word.

3. At the prompt, type the word you want. If the word is a headword, the Thesaurus displays the word with all its subgroups of synonyms and antonyms. If the word is not a headword, WordPerfect either looks up a similar word or displays the message * Word Not Found *. You can press F1 (Cancel) or look up another word.

Upper- and Lowercase

WordPerfect can change whole words, sentences, paragraphs, or documents to upper- or lowercase letters automatically. This feature is useful when you discover that you typed a section of text with Caps Lock on.

To change to upper- or lowercase letters

1. Position the cursor at the beginning of the section.

2. Press Alt-F4 (Block) or F12.

3. Move the cursor to the end of the text.

4. Press Shift-F3 (Switch).

5. Press 1 or U to change to uppercase letters or press 2 or L to change to lowercase letters.

After the highlighted text changes case, the Switch menu disappears.

Note

Because WordPerfect recognizes the first word of a sentence and the pronoun *I*, they remain capitalized when you select lowercase. To ensure that WordPerfect recognizes the block is a sentence, include the preceding sentence's ending punctuation when you define your block of text.

Windows

WordPerfect's two document windows give you essentially two areas within which to work. The status line tells you whether the Doc 1 or the Doc 2 window is the active workspace. The cursor's position determines whether the window is active.

You can type in both windows and switch back and forth. Initially, each window is the entire size of the screen. You can split the screen to look at two documents or at different parts of the same document.

Reminders

When you display two documents, you lose two lines of the screen. These lost lines are used by an additional status line and a ruler line.

Before you split the screen, decide how many lines you want to display in the current document. The other document will take what is left.

To switch between document windows

1. Press Shift-F3 (Switch).

2. To switch back to the Doc 1 window, press Shift-F3 (Switch) again.

To split the screen

1. Press Ctrl-F3 (Screen).

2. Press 1 for Window.

3. Type 11, or use ↑ and ↓, and then press Enter.

Your screen should be split in half, with WordPerfect's tab ruler line displayed across the middle.

To resize the window to a full-screen display

1. Press Ctrl-F3 (Screen).

2. Press 1 or W for Window.

3. At the prompt asking for the number of lines in the window, type 24 and press Enter.

Caution: Never retrieve the same file into both windows. If you do and then edit in both windows, only the changes made in last version saved remain intact.

Index